ESTABLISHED IN 1973

PUBLISHED QUARTERLY
by Berea College
CPO 2166
205 N. Main Street
Berea, KY, 40404

Telephone: 859.985.3559
Facsimile: 859.985.3903
Email: appalachianheritage@berea.edu
www.appalachianheritage.net

EDITOR
Jason Howard

STUDENT ASSISTANTS
Cheyenne Bridgewater & Dylan Mullins

©2014 by Berea College. Vol. 42, No. 3, Summer 2014. All rights reserved. No part of this publication may be reproduced without the prior permission of *Appalachian Heritage*. Periodicals postage paid at Berea, Kentucky, and at additional mailing offices. ISSN# 03632318.

The short stories in this publication are works of fiction. Names, characters, places, and incidents are either the products of the authors' imaginations or are used fictitiously. Any resemblance to actual events, locales, or persons, living or dead, is entirely coincidental. The views expressed in the creative nonfiction herein are solely those of the authors.

Electronic submissions only at www.appalachianheritage.net

Distributed by the University of North Carolina Press. Basic subscription price: $30/year for individuals, $40/year for institutions. For subscription requests and inquiries, visit the magazine's website, email uncpress_journals@unc.edu, or call 919.962.4201.

CONTENTS

CRAFT ESSAY

SPECIAL FEATURE: LITERARY EXPLORATION

BOOK REVIEWS

ILLUSTRATIONS

EDITOR'S NOTE

JASON HOWARD

At the beginning of the year, one of my dear friends, whom I believe to be one of the best readers I know, started a Facebook campaign. Each day she collects a book—driving to purchase one from a bookshop in nearby Owensboro, ordering one online, or culling one from her deceased mother's collection that remains in storage. "Today's Accumulated Book," she labels her posts, and two hundred days into the year, she has amassed a library of varying genres and quality.

On the literary side, there is Thomas Merton's *The Seven Storey Mountain,* Jesse Graves's latest poetry collection *Basin Ghosts,* even an advance reader's copy of Marilynne Robinson's *Lila*—a book that my friend went to great trouble and online investigation to accumulate. There is the whimsical—*100 Favorite Songs for the Ukelele* (my friend doesn't play) and *Betty Crocker's Picture Cook Book* (she makes some fine country ham and biscuits). And then there are the guilty pleasures, including *Little Gloria...Happy at Last*—a biography of Gloria Vanderbilt—and Howard Fast's *The Establishment,* which chronicles the marriage trials of a former socialite and a poor mechanic.

I look forward to reading my friend's posts each day, wondering what kind of book she will collect, and I often reflect on how much the volumes mean to her, both individually and collectively. They are family members, treasured companions with which she has formed a relationship. In doing so, she agrees with writer and teacher Richard Hague, who observes in his book *Lives of the Poem,* "Poems are living things. And because they are living things, the same degree of attentiveness and the same diligence and tolerance and creativity necessary to establishing and maintaining human friendships are necessary to developing a friendship with poetry."

It goes without saying that Hague's statement, although focused on poetry, also relates to other literary genres. To be a good reader—and certainly a writer—one must have a deep, abiding love of words, of a particularly lyrical phrase, of a moving character and gripping narrative.

In this issue, I predict you will find stories, essays, and poems with which you will form a close bond. You will be absorbed by James Braziel's story "Watersmeet," A.W. Marshall's "Foundered," and Leah Hampton's "Queen." You will marvel at Sonja Livingston's mastery of form in her lyric essay "Blue Kentucky Girl." You will be moved by the rhythm and images found in the poetry of Pauletta Hansel, Samantha Lynn Cole, and others included here. You will ponder on the musings of George Ella Lyon and Erica Abrams Locklear in their essays on craft and literary theme, and you will be intrigued by the thoughts of Richard Hague, whose interview is featured in this issue.

In his beautiful play *Shadowlands,* which depicts the tragic love story of British writer C.S. Lewis and American poet Joy Davidman, William Nicholson has Lewis muse, "We read to know we're not alone."

I leave you now to make some new friends. ■

WATERSMEET

JAMES BRAZIEL

There's a ridge I need to climb ever since Toadman died. He loved toads. Got his nickname that way. Always hanging out with them and brushing the splotches on their backs like the splotches were grey pools of lily pad hair. Toadman and I biked and walked to every creek in the county for we are not a county of rivers, just rills and rivulets widening into creeks. I followed because he knew where the frogs hid in summer on the cool north banks beneath mud funks and old pine logs that had tumbled down. He found a copperhead like that once. Got bit straight through his wading thumb.

See, Toadman always put his wading thumb in first cause the other frogs thought it was a fellow frog. He never wanted them to be afraid. Copperhead thought he had come upon a fellow frog, too. One moment Toadman was combing the water quiet, next he was hollering louder than the coyotes beyond Zeller Hoyt's place at four in the morning when you can't sleep and wish you could. Toadman's hand zipped up and the snake wiggled off. It splashed down a beautiful pipe-copper-rain. I unplugged my boots from the shallows to help, but the fangs had torn through the front and come out back busting Toadman's nail off the bed. Every time I pressed the nail down, it popped up. Blood oozed out. His thumb throbbed.

"You my best friend," Toadman said. First time he'd ever said it, like he better say what was on his mind quick. His face swirled in a pink fuzzy sweat.

I told him straight out, "You ain't dying, Brother." He was not my real brother but a brother in that other way, truer to claim someone and no blood between you. We was kids then, and in that moment I meant what I said, and he meant what he said. You think when you say certain things, they last forever, as if our atoms will never change, as if certain words when spoken right might actually become real. It ain't so. I promise, all you hold as true and forever is not.

"When I die, do me one favor."

"You ain't going to die."

"Cut my thumb off, Beal. Put it in at The Cross, so it grows into a frog." He put his thumb in my face.

“You’re talking crazy,” I said. Toadman was somewhat of a magical thinker, but cutting his thumb? A thumb turning into a frog? A thumb pretending to be a frog was one thing, but—

“Promise,” he yelled. Yelled.

People get delusional. I knew that even then, especially with the sun burning hot like it was. I said, “All right now. All right,” to calm him down. “But you ain’t dying,” I added, though I was none too sure. He was turning white like all the blood had already gone out his thumb and the hollowed vessels were ready to carry the poison deep. Any moment, his hand would swell like a balloon until it burst, but that’s not what happened.

We scaled the top of Hanna Ridge, shuffled down the other side to the highway. We had walked here, four miles from our homes. The highway was Bull’s Holler and not much traffic to speak of.

“Shouldn’t you put a turnip on my arm?” He held his arm out, waiting for the venom to crawl. I couldn’t decipher turnip-on-my-arm.

“You know,” he said louder after my longish silence, “to keep the juice in my thumb. Make the venom stay put.”

“Tourniquet,” I said. I knew that word from my brother who volunteered for Blount Fire and Rescue and had put a tourniquet on an injured man once. He always gave me his stories of saving others.

“Oh, yeah, *that*,” Toadman said and counted the broken yellow lines on the highway. Nothing worse than feeling you’re not smart enough. But before he said that Oh I thought maybe he did mean turnip, some witchy thing he might do like his wading thumb, like his brushing the invisible hairs on the big fat lily toads, which made them bend their legs into his hand. They appreciated what he did, how he held them.

“I think you got a dry bite.” I pointed to his oozing thumb which looked as if it’d been smashed by a hammer knocking down two nails. Dry bite was another one of my brother's phrases. "But I'll put a tourniquet on you just to be sure." I pulled off my shirt, knotted it, sweat-drenched it around his arm above the elbow.

He was still breathing hard from our up-and-over Hanna. Both of us had fallen on the brown pine needles wet from yesterday's rain.

Truth is, I didn't know if he had a dry bite or not, but I wanted Toadman to relax.

I made the knot tight.

He nodded at me and I at him like best friends and brothers do. We walked up Bull's Holler, caught a ride to the hospital, a fellow out of Allgood, I didn't know. And Toadman was perfectly okay.

"You have no venom. Not a drop."

"Are you sure?" he asked the doctor more than once.

"None." The doctor smiled. "You've been lucky today, young man. A dry bite." The doctor wore a long white coat. All the walls and nurses and equipment and lights gave off the same unyielding milky color. Toadman's parents hadn't shown up

I inhaled my first full breath since the snake waggled off Toadman's thumb, and I started on a hiccup jag that lasted over an hour.

yet when we were told this. No one could find them. But even without the reassurances of parents, we were relieved.

I inhaled my first full breath since the snake waggled off Toadman's thumb, and I started on a hiccup jag that lasted over an hour.

The room was so white, it hurt to take all of it in. Like the inside of the sun if you could peel back its orange to the center, let spill out the hot blinding seeds.

■ ■ ■

This ridge I need to climb isn't Hanna. It's Osanippa, the tallest in the county. You have to come up from Bull's Holler, then up-and-over Hanna, to Switchback, which takes you on to Osanippa. Follow the crest line to a sheer rock drop. Look over the edge. Below is the place we call The Cross, which is where all our creeks come together—Foot, Sally Branch, Big, Pike, and Luna—to make the start of the Locust Fork.

The waterways layout like a compass, which you can see atop Osanippa. For a long time, I wanted to take a girl up there. No one in particular, but I like brown hair, and for hips to sway like loose brown curls, for her to want me coming in close without hesitation.

Water's two necks high at The Cross. From Sally and Foot the water spits out a sand beach every spring. Most people come in that way to smooch or have a beer party. But some have perished jumping off Osanippa, slammed their heads into the rock slick bottom and broke their necks just like that. My brother said just like that with the snap of his fingers while telling stories of the drunk bodies he'd pulled out: Todd Chastain—*Lips torn off by catfish*; Chester Rounds—*No ears after we trawled him out from under the rapids. Funeral parlor broke his bones to set him in his casket right;* and the one girl, Maya Maya. My brother never gave anything away about her. Whenever he spoke her name, he shook his head and drew his breath in like he wanted her back. But double names are rare and easy to remember.

Some people claim to have made the jump and lived. When the water's rushing high—that's the key they say. If you're not too tall—that helps, too. But the biggest key is if you know how to float down like a feather, not fall like a rock. Use the air to hold you up so by the time you cut through those ribbons of water, you won't go in far. *Water,* Tanya Preston who supposedly made the jump and who isn't tall, explained to a group of us at Saterfield's once, *Water is just heavy air, ribbons of heavy air. Think of it, she said, that way.*

I've dreamed it that way—how my body might could float and fall, a strong crosswind lifting my elbows and ankles. Once down in the cool wet, my fat legs and arms bubbled me up to the surface. In one dream I knotted a kite to myself, naked, and slipped, just slipped right into the water. So easy. All of that from the tallest place in the county, from where you can spy on the world further than normally you're able.

■ ■ ■

For the rest of that summer, Toadman and I kept going to the north banks for frogs. He used his other thumb but without as much success. Turns out, his right wasn't born a frog. Then we started back to school and found other best friends, other brothers to be around.

I call those days The Before Time. Like they do in the Bible. Only my brother is the marker in my story. His name was Junius, but everyone called him June. The Before Time happened before June rushed in on a trailer thinking someone was inside. He shouldered the door down. With just that little extra push of air, the fire caught huge and hot. He had run in like a furious train. But it was his ashes, no one else's, found once things cooled.

I have looked after my mother since then. This is The After Time. Her thoughts are still tangled up with June's death and cannot untangle. Most days, she digs her nails into her palms until they bleed and says his name and my father's name who passed not long after I was born. I didn't know him except that he was called Fleet. In the morning she says, "Good morning, Fleet," to me.

“I’m not him,” I have to tell her. “Sorry I can’t be your man today.” Sometimes I say yes to give her comfort. She grabs my shoulders then, hoping to rub them into his skin-over-bones. But my shoulders are all wrong because when she rubs, that’s when she knows I’m lying.

“Well, when Fleet gets here, he’ll know what.”

Or she says, “I wish your brother’d come for dinner,” and trail off because she can’t place either of them outside herself into the small length of world she wanders through. By lunch she’s doing her nervous digging. I can’t pry her nails up until she naps. That’s when I cup her hands, pour peroxide over the wounds. They froth a brown scabby blood. She flinches but doesn’t wake as I dab the puss-froth clean.

Lots of people have died I don’t care about. Live long enough and you’ll close yourself from others, too. I didn’t care about my brother as much as I should’ve. There was a big difference in our ages and he only let me into his world when he wanted, controlling what it was of him, I might take. But when Toadman passed, that was different. Maybe it was the way he passed, shot by his own father, or maybe that we had that one summer together catching big frogs which I enjoyed more than anything else I’ve done, or maybe that I saved his life once, which turned out not to be enough, which turned out to be at the time a mere dry bite and not as big a deal. I had made a promise to him then. And a promise to a dead brother is one you keep.

■ ■ ■

Happened one of those afternoons riding around with June drinking beer, the wind just howling, punching the doors of the truck as we squiggled down wet clay roads. I wasn’t twelve yet, but he had started to let me drink just to get the taste, which I hated, but wanting to be a big man, I kept sipping tiny on that rotten wood water. It was winter. We drove around the county in his Silverado to look at different places he hunted. Sometimes we parked to check on his stands. During the driving part, we inspected the clay ditches for deer trails. During an earlier excursion, in an alluvial fan, we found panther tracks. My brother was always talking about some big buck—a sixteen pointer he had hunted forever. Lived up in the Alapaha where no one lived. And now there was a panther to hunt in the Alapaha, too.

On this day my brother got a call to help carry a body down. A hunting accident. A boy shot by his own father in the woods near Double Run. The Ashburn side of the spur. Sheriff Pinkie Sligh—his crazy name gets him half his votes, I swear—was with state troopers and Alabama Power on 131 where a semi

I wasn't twelve yet, but he had started to let me drink just to get the taste, which I hated, but wanting to be a big man, I kept sipping...

had run off the road into a pole. Driver had nodded off and was dead. Electricity knocked out for miles. Since Pinkie wore many hats—he was also Chief of Blount Fire and Rescue—he called my brother to help with the shooting until Pinkie could get done.

"No problem. I'll get there," my brother said.

"He just walked off the ridge down to the road. Oweda Gillam's mother, Tess, found him in her yard, wandering in circles. I mean, he didn't even try to bring his kid out. Would you've done that?" I heard that much from my brother's phone and leaned closer to hear more.

"The man's in shock, Pinkie."

"Tess keeps calling every five minutes for someone to remove him from her yard. She won't let him in the house. Oweda's with some new boy in Gatlinburg. No help at all, that girl. You know their place?"

"I know it," my brother said and said goodbye. Then my brother said to me, "We've got something to do, Little." Little was my nickname because, as he put it, I was little compared to him. And at the time, that was true.

I straightened up. "What's going on?" I wanted to get rid of the beer before we arrived at this place of eventual sheriffs and ambulances, but my brother kept pushing the gas so hard I was afraid to crack open the door. What if the door shot open and pulled me onto the pavement? I always thought of the worst ways to die. Too cold to let the window down. So I drank my last swallows of wood piss quick. "Someone hurt?"

"You know the Lace boy? About your age."

"Toadman?" I said.

"Toadman?" My brother's mouth turned like he'd just eaten turned meat.

"Evan," I said. "Evan Lace."

"Yeah, him." My brother wiggled around to move his hands better on the wheel. If someone'd been coming around those dirt road corners they'd be dead.

"Well?"

■ ■ ■

I'm heading out, decision made, not driving, going to walk Bull's Holler like it should be done, and from there Osanippa. We've had lots of rain and one ice storm so far this winter, but today has been a February thawer, the sun out good, and whatever cold the ground has held onto, it's having to give back to the air, which is glad to take it and sweep that cold far, far up into the sky. A windy day. Southerly, coming off the Gulf with lots of crossing. I've got my knife—my brother's Buck. In my left pocket, I have the thumb.

Not Toadman's. He passed when I was almost twelve and I'm twenty-two now. His thumb is all worm-eaten-ash. I've survived in The After Time without my brother for years. No, that thumb belongs to someone found on Zeller Hoyt's place five days ago.

Let me back up—we've had a run of murders, and we're not a county that has murders. Or murderers, for that matter. But for the last year, about every two months, a body is found on the side of the highway, or behind someone's house, or, and this was the strangest place yet, five days ago someone got wrapped up in one of Zeller Hoyt's barbed-wire fences.

Strange part is, the bodies are headless, footless and handless. They carry no identification. That's what Sheriff Pinkie Sligh has focused on. Someone is murdering people to take their driver's licenses and cards, to steal their identity, then leaving no way for the authorities to figure out who the dead are—no hands, no feet, no teeth. And the killer, or killers, are dumping the bodies in our part of Alabama because we're in the middle of Jesus Christ nowhere. Where they come from? Probably drug smugglers out of Orleans. We haven't had a rash of missing persons in the county, so the folks we find are from somewhere else. That much we know.

At Zeller Hoyt's I found a hand—I'm a volunteer, took my brother's place once I got old enough—and the killer, or killers, had cut it loose and lost it. Must have fallen from their satchel. Which is all that squares because with the hand, the body could be identified. Only, I kept it.

Some people puke when they come upon these brutalized bodies. Maybe they see themselves torn up or they place onto the figures the figure of someone they love. But my stomach doesn't rattle. When I found the hand at the tree line, blood-sticky and palish, I thought . . . I don't know what I was thinking, really. But I wanted it, so I hushed it under pine needles and later came back, wiped the needles off. I've kept the hand outside in a Ziploc bag, which I know is crazy. I should've taken it to Sheriff Pinkie Sligh, and at this point, I've put myself in a situation, cause they're going to wonder about me. But yesterday as I turned the bruised fingers round, barely able to get them to flex through the plastic, I thought of my promise to Toadman.

I did what had to be done—I cut the thumb loose, sawed clean down the jointed bone and washed it and burned the rest in a barrel-fire...

I know it's not Toadman's, and I know my actions are pure craziness, but earlier this morning, I did what had to be done—I cut the thumb loose, sawed clean down the jointed bone and washed it and burned the rest in a barrel-fire with the trash I burn every Saturday. Mother's up. She's been fed. I'm heading to Osanippa.

■ ■ ■

When we got to Oweda Gilliam's place, Toadman's father was chicken walking, going in circles in the large yard of black seed bahia that kept curling under the wind, the yard that touches the Ashburn Highway. He had a shotgun. Tess was secured behind her window in a robe, clutching a phone.

"You stay in the truck, Little," my brother said. The door slammed and he called, "Mr. Lace."

Toadman's father stopped and circled the other way, away from my brother.

"I know this isn't good. But we have to go up and get your son. If you—"

But Toadman's father wasn't paying attention. He was in a circling trance.

"Come on, Mr. Lace," my brother said, keeping back. I hadn't realized it, but I had sunk down, my eyes just over the metal door the wind kept pounding on. I was ready to duck even further into the seat and spilled coffee and beer on the floor, where the warmth of the truck had dwindled with the heater off. Then my brother, he just walked up to Toadman's father and grabbed the barrel, stopped the man from walking.

"I'm taking this." That broke Mr. Lace's spell. You have to understand, my brother was big, train big, and when he took hold of things, he didn't let go until ready. But I thought maybe Toadman's father would fight my brother. A fight he would lose, but when people get delusional, they do hurtful things.

"Why you here?" Mr. Lace said.

"To help," my brother said. He pointed to the window. "Tess called Sheriff Pinkie Sligh. He sent me and my brother." My brother pointed to the truck. "I'm Junius Chambers. My father was Fleet Chambers."

"Marvelle your mother?"

"She is," my brother said.

"I remember when your father passed." Mr. Lace stared at the ground, which in our county is a sign of respect for the dead.

"So do I. Now let's go get your son."

But Mr. Lace didn't budge, and Tess moved away from her window for good.

I should be out there. If he saw me and recognized me as his son's friend, maybe that would help the situation. I took the door handle. *One more second, in you go,* I said to myself, kept saying it, but Toadman's father nodded a chicken nod and saved me from my heroics. He let go his weapon.

June put the shotgun in the truck rack above his rifle and grabbed his revolver from behind the seat. A small .22 full of hollow points, which could, if called upon, bring damage to a body. My brother by his size and weight alone could bring damage, but he kept that .22 for practice on the beer cans we finished off. He had let me shoot it a few times, so I understood how. It had belonged to our father, milk-handled, silver.

"What happened to Toadman?"

"Get out," he said and shoved the revolver in his back pocket. He said to Toadman's father over the cab. "You got to take us where your son is. Going to take all three of us to carry

I knew then something bad had happened, but I wasn't sure what. Maybe I didn't want to know.

him down."

"I'm not sure where it is exactly. The place." He huffed like no way he'd ever catch his breath right. Toadman had breathed like that after the copperhead struck his thumb. I knew then something bad had happened, but I wasn't sure what. Maybe I didn't want to know. Something in me, however, wanted to shake that man until he said where Toadman was. Something else in my shoulders and legs started to fall back. That's when my brother held me with his eyes, that look saying, don't fall apart now, Little.

"If you can get us near," my brother said. "Retrace as best you can, all right?"

But Mr. Lace wouldn't respond, so my brother said, "We have to get Evan now."

And that's when Toadman's father stopped huffing. He paused like before, then chicken nodded. Funny how someone's name can stop you, whatever motion you're in, and suddenly that someone is right in front of your brain, right behind your eyes, gesturing for you to come closer.

Toadman's father looked my way for the first time, yet it was like he'd never known me. Maybe he couldn't remember—it had been over a year since I was at his house—or maybe it was just the shock of his son's death, but from what I could tell of him, he wasn't someone I recognized at all.

■ ■ ■

How my father died—got a tattoo at Tugbail's, which got infected. Worse than that, he got tetanus and his body swole until it broke. That's the story my brother gave. My mother will tell me nothing of it.

My brother got a tattoo once. Of a hawk, right on his arm, right where you could see. My mother got angry at him. She kept saying, *What'd you do that for? Why you do that, Junius?* She kept her arms crossed. Uncrossing them only to pick at stray curls on her head.

"Had to," he told her.

I got so mad, I punched him right in the tattoo. Wanted to make that blue-green hawk fly.

My brother grabbed my head. For a second I thought he had snapped my head out of its socket. But he told me, "Punch it, again, Little."

So I whumped that hawk harder and harder like I could break through to the flesh, get inside the belly of the hawk, the arm of my brother—they were one in the same—only then would I stop. And my brother, it had to hurt him some cause the way his mouth turned. Yet all he said once I stopped throwing punches, too tired to throw anymore— "See, Little, see. I'm alive. So very much alive."

■ ■ ■

We found the place where Toadman was, and my brother took his shotgun, clicked the shells out clean. He told me to put the shells in my pocket. I fumbled them on my pocket's lip. Somehow they didn't fall. So I stuffed my pockets full, and June handed the gun over before I could whimper.

Flat on the ground, face up, was someone I had called my brother once. Only he no longer looked scared like he had that

The tops of the pines bowed how the wind wanted, like if they bowed down enough they might not stay put and instead spring up, shoot the cold air and the clouds far into the sky.

summer afternoon. Death makes the difference. Death had carried away his fear.

My brother asked Toadman's father what happened.

"We were walking down the ridge. Gun shot my boy in the back. Was an accident."

The tops of the pines bowed how the wind wanted, like if they bowed down enough they might not stay put and instead spring up, shoot the cold air and the clouds far into the sky. But the cold kept coming at us, the wind pushing it.

My brother held Toadman's neck for a pulse, then lifted his body slightly at the shoulders, the ankles. Already it was like the body wasn't my friend, just a shell. His heart had stopped hours ago. The leaves and dirt had soaked up all his blood. That promise of the dry bite had come true.

What would the bite feel like now, I wondered? Maybe the healed scars were in place or maybe when he passed, all his wounds opened up, again. I hadn't known a dead body except for TV, so I made up my own stories about what death could do, what happened to a body after. But I was holding the shotgun like my brother wanted and could not raise up that hand to see.

My brother tapped a wide hole on Toadman's chest, which is what my brother did whenever he found the bullet wounds on deer he killed.

"Came in that way?" I said it like a question.

My brother looked up, holding the air between us to make it silent because he understood things quicker than me.

"Let's take him down," he said to Mr. Lace. "I'll take the arms, each of you the legs."

But Mr. Lace had heard what I said. My first mistake. At least I think that was it. Or maybe it was my brother tapping near the hole in the chest. Or maybe it was just Mr. Lace's lie couldn't hold him together any longer. The man started running to the top of the ridge. This one's name was Younger Ridge.

My brother grabbed a shell out of my pocket, pulled the chamber open, clicked it in, and handed the shotgun back. All of this happened so fast that the stock and barrel, where I'd been holding the gun was still warm from where I had held it before, where I was holding it now. Time jumbled up on itself. I didn't know what to do.

"You stay with Evan," he said. "If you need this." He took the safety off. I said nothing.

"You know how," my brother said. "Just like the .22," he said. I nodded. And he stepped into the trees, running.

■ ■ ■

So I climb. All morning. Up-and-over Hanna. Across the sideways paths that mark Switchback, the sky turning blue until there's no more grey to filter out. The wind pushes me up and up until that mile of Osanippa is done. And I'm here. The highest point in the county. Straight down is The Cross where all our waters meet. First the rains. The rains funnel along rills and rivulets into wider and still wider pathways carrying off our iron dirt, our rocks, our dead branches. This place is where everything in the county eventually comes from one direction or another. This place is where everything vanishes from us.

The water is high today, swirling and clear to the pebbled bottom. In the center of The Cross, a smooth mossed rock juts out. The water laps at it like the rock is a dog's thirsty tongue and its thirsty heart.

The thumb is ready to become a frog if, just for a few seconds, I can have Toadman's magical thinking. I'm ready. But there's one last thing to tell.

■ ■ ■

"You know how," my brother said. I nodded.

Sometimes you can make one mistake and get away with it. But seldom two. I wasn't thinking fast like my brother, or maybe, no, the opposite, I thought too fast, wanting to compensate for being almost twelve, for not knowing enough, and I set my finger at the trigger ready because Toadman's father, he'd be back—his legs running in reverse flickered on my brain pan—he'd come here, and I'd have to stop him from getting away with whatever he'd done, which, turned out was shoot Toadman over fallen branches in their yard. That was all. Walking down the ridge, having not shot one deer or quail, Mr. Lace said that Toadman had to gather branches as soon as they got home to make the yard respectable. Yesterday's storm had brought the branches down.

Toadman had a terrarium in his room with turtles. He had a rabbit. And he wanted to see about them.

All that summer we were brothers, I came over to his house. His family kept the AC on, and I shivered walking inside. My family had no AC money. Their living room smelled of sweet grease and sugar tea, good smells, but his room had the odor of soured wood. The turtles and rabbit, however, didn't seem to mind, so I didn't mind.

"Where the frogs?" I asked. He never kept any of the frogs we found.

"If I bring something, I have to let something here go," he said. "That's Lenore, Anna, and Lulu." He pointed to the biggest turtle, a black shell crossed in yellow lines, then the smaller one, then the rabbit. He told me this on my first visit.

"But you could keep as many frogs as you want," I said.

"It'd get too crowded," Toadman said and I thought of the sour wood. My brother had said pets were nothing but thankless work. "Besides, I like letting things out of their cage."

"You're going to pick up the branches," is what his father told him as they walked down Younger Ridge. "We're not talking about this anymore. When we get back, you'll do what I tell you."

Toadman said something—he cussed his father. Or maybe he just said No. But whatever he said made his father turn, raise his shotgun and shoot Toadman, point blank, in the chest. Just like that. Point blank. And he loved his son. Loved his son very much.

And me, I was set on the trigger, ready for Mr. Lace. But off it went and shot my brother, just like that, as he turned.

I said something, but my eardrums had popped, and the wind, myself, and my brother had all become hushed. So I tried to hold his side where I'd hit him, put what had fallen out of him back.

He kept saying to call Pinkie. Said that in short breaths.

The blood poured through my hands in the pulse of those breaths.

"Call," he said until the words spiraled down into my ears and took.

"I'm sorry," I said because my fingers kept sticking to the numbers and I mashed the wrong ones until eventually, I got through.

"I'm not good," June said. "Been shot. Little didn't mean—I'm the one gave him the gun, all right?" His tone shifted. "Get up here. Mr. Lace has run off. Follow the firebreak. Just get here."

My brother said Pinkie was on his way and to keep the phone close and then he directed me on putting another shell in the chamber. "Watch for Mr. Lace," he said. "Don't be afraid," he said. "Promise."

I promised.

It wasn't even the last half of the afternoon. The clouds had left and there was a lot of light. I started to worry the darkness would come before they found us. Nothing in the stories my brother had told me, nothing helped me save him. But before he passed, I called, "You still there?" whenever he got quiet and waited for a response.

"Over here, Little," he said, like he said when we played in our yard at night, and I couldn't find him. T*ell me where you are, please,* I'd say after a while of spinning, grabbing at the dark and never him, catching no moths, nothing, losing my own breath. *I'm about to fall,* I'd warn. Gravity had put an ache through my head. But before I smacked the earth, he looped his arms round my waist and held me off the ground and laughed, shaking me in that laugh, saying, *I got you, Little. I got you good.* That sudden stop brought a rush to my head, which brought light to my eyes the curl and color of lightning yellow. For a second, he had pushed the dark away, and I brushed my fingers over the dirt and grass and the round ends of his boots until he righted me.

"Over here, Little," he said like he had said in the yard or he groaned, or he murmured words I couldn't put together. I netted my hands tighter against the wound to make the best patch until my arms ached and fell. The blood turned cold and sticky in the wind. On my tongue, gunpowder and metal. I wanted water. The sun stayed on us, not moving it seemed.

"You still there?" I called, but time wasn't working right.

Mr. Lace had disappeared. If my brother had gone after him—my brother wasn't made for running, I can tell you that. Like a train, he'd do good coming down a ridge. You wouldn't want to get in his way. But going up would've been too hard.

I thought of my father's revolver, the hollow points, how they busted beer cans. But it wasn't until later when Sheriff Pinkie Sligh showed up and took us down and the dogs cornered Mr. Lace that it struck me, like an axe spinning right through the center, what I'd done.

■ ■ ■

My brother didn't die in a fire. Though sometimes I tell the story that way. But even when I tell the other story to make myself know it, the truth is not quite the truth no matter how much you need it to be, no matter how much of it you tell. Too many other things got lost that afternoon, and the truth can't hold it all.

An accident. A murder. It's been a long time since I've had a brother to drive around the county with, slip along the north banks with. A long time since my brother gave me a story of rescuing, though his voice is in my head. Some things do not die. And a long time, too, since Toadman combed the water with his frog-thumb. I stood with my shoes half in the mud, my body so still, waiting for that moment when a frog made a swimming leap out from under a hiding place. Every time one did, it was a miracle. And I was right there. A part of it. ■

DIANA

Slade Kentucky, ca. 1975

In her dreams, she sees rabbits
running in the woods.

White ones swallow black
ones, head first and whole.

She labors to push them out
before they stop

breathing. In her mind,
she has infinite children

with cherub faces.
They bring her what they kill.

She eats the hearts first,
before they go bad—

as all hearts will.

JESSICA D. THOMPSON

CHASING BEAUTY

She takes up too much space
with her books, her soup

bowls. Breaks a bone
rather than cope

with brokenness.
There are so many ways to do it:

pistol, razor blade, river.
But she can't accept

the ugliness, the spectacle—
when all her life

she has chased after beauty.
So she starts keeping bees,

growing plots of Oleander
because she read somewhere

that their flowers
will poison you

if you eat the honey
made by bees

that have savored the nectar.

JESSICA D. THOMPSON

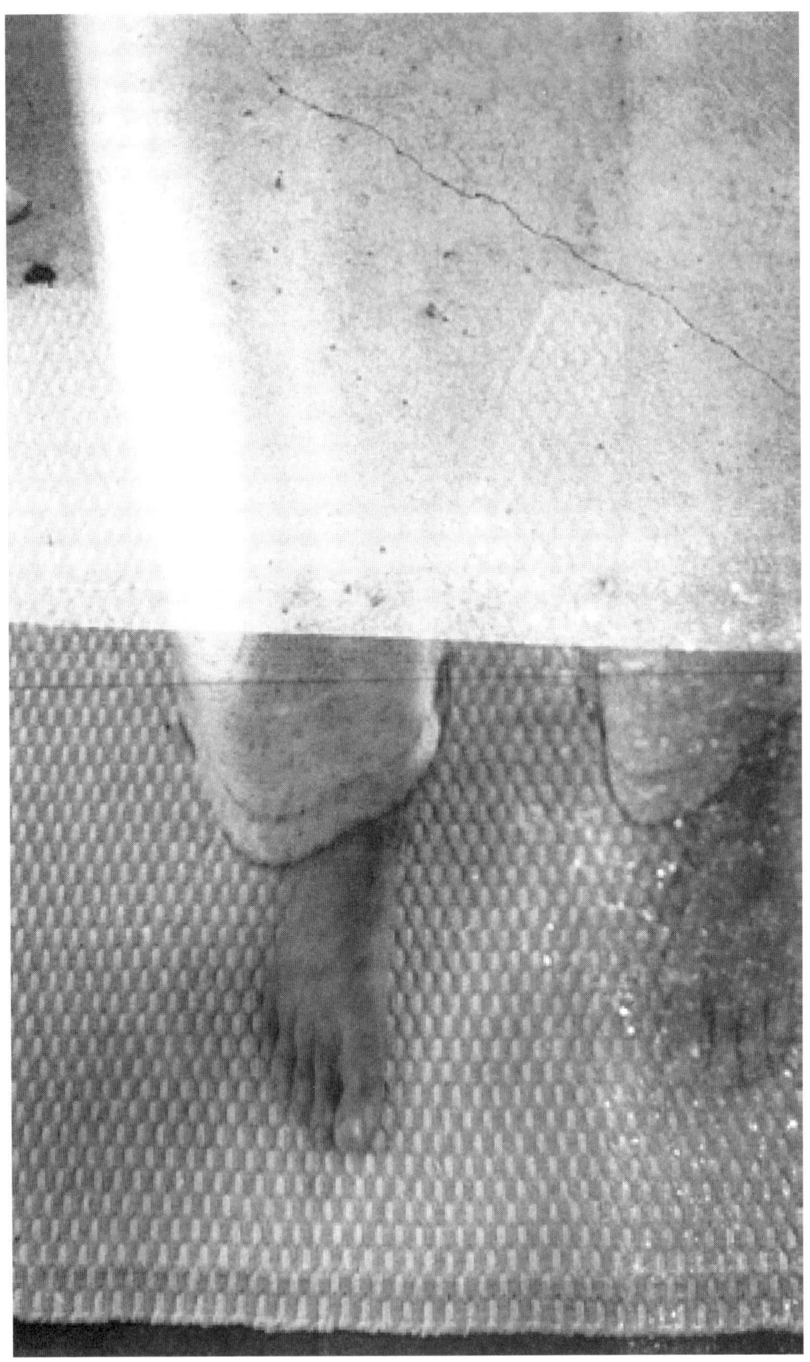

BLUE KENTUCKY GIRL

SONJA LIVINGSTON

Named for the moon. Little Luna. Luna, blue. The details surrounding your birth are murky, some say 1878, others say a decade later, but why squabble over a handful of years? What's most clear is that by the time you were born in eastern Kentucky, people had settled into its isolated pockets, inhabiting hollows along the Cumberland Plateau, fringed by rocky ridges and ravines. Men cut timber for as many hours as they could stand, women tended children and planted corn and potatoes wherever they could clear rocks from the soil, the hardness of their lives contrasted by a world bursting with waterfall and fern. Into this world, little ones came, replacing fathers and mothers, child, boys and girls for the shortest of time, and one of them, near the end of the century was you. Born into the Fugate family, the one I call out to, little Luna blue.

■ ■ ■

Your mama would have been raised on stories of Fugates going back to the time Troublesome Creek was settled in the 1820s. She would have known a few of your daddy's strangely-tinted cousins, would have spent time with an indigo-skinned niece. She'd married a Fugate after all, and in the isolated hills of eastern Kentucky, there was so much intermarriage that even she carried a spot of Fugate blood. Known as the blue people of Kentucky, people talked of them for miles. But what did that have to do with your mama? Mahala Fugate's skin was white, as was her husband's, and all of her other babies, each of which had unfolded from her soft and pink as wild azalea blossoms.

■ ■ ■

Most babies born with Fugate blood were as pale as every other white child in eastern Kentucky. Even among Fugates, it was rare to stay blue. Most of those who showed a tinge upon birth lost their color after a few weeks, a fact Mahala must have repeated to herself as she cradled you, dear Luna, whose skin was like a stain against her breast. Families had to scrounge to survive those hills, so Mahala couldn't have afforded much time to worry, though being different is nothing anyone ever courted. Life was hard enough without the burden of strangely colored skin. How your mama must have lifted the edge of her blanket to check on you again and again, listening hard to those around her, clinging to the clucking of old aunts and her husband's reassurances. *Just give it time*, they'd have said, *that young'un's skin will right itself, fade as fast as the passing of the days.*

But the days passed, then passed again, and you remained the bluest of all babies born at Troublesome Creek, blue as the gentians growing along the creeks, bluer than even the moon you were named for.

■ ■ ■

A blue moon itself isn't as rare as it might seem. Two full moons in one month, it happens once, and sometimes even twice, a year. *Once in a blue moon*, people say, and what they mean is *hardly ever*. The saying began as a way to speak not so much of a rarity, but of an absurdity, an occurrence as unlikely as hell freezing over, as impossible as child in the hills of Kentucky, gathering flowers whose color mirrors her face. And even that is only pretty thinking. No, the lips on your face would have been more like the patches of denim your mama sewed to your daddy's broken trousers than the color of springtime blossoms. Once in a blue moon. Hardly ever. And then along came you.

■ ■ ■

Commonly known as met-H, *methaemoglobinaemia* is a disorder that results in the reduced ability to carry oxygen in the blood. As a result, the blood of those affected is made darker, so much so, that the darkened blood tints the skin blue, which is known as cyanosis, or the "blue disease." The condition is usually caused by environmental factors, such as reactions to certain drugs and exposure to nitrates and dyes. But in rare cases, blue-skin can be congenital, as in the case of the Fugates, whose randomly aligned alleles combined with chance and geographic isolation to produce blue people in Troublesome Creek for more than a hundred years.

■ ■ ■

So many blues in Kentucky. The heads of grasses. The Bluegrass state, its music, the picking and banjos, the voices calling out from the lonesome hills. Its moon, looming large in the sky, making the night its very own shade. Sung of by Bill Monroe (*Blue moon of Kentucky, keep on shining*) and again by Patsy Cline, and Elvis, the boy who sang another

But the days passed, then passed again, and you remained the bluest of all babies born at Troublesome Creek...

song about the Blue Moon: *you saw me standing alone, without a dream in my heart.* And that should be enough, but there's Kentucky's best known daughter, Loretta Lynn, who came from a hollow not too far from Luna, and who sang with her sad strong voice: *just come on home to your blue Kentucky girl.*

■ ■ ■

Blue as a bruise, was said of the lips on Luna Fugate's face. *Blue all over. As blue a woman as I ever saw.*

■ ■ ■

The dates of your life are jumbled, but no matter what math is used, you were still a girl when spotted by an admirer while attending services at the Baptist Church. Perhaps something grabbed him as you sang a hymn, perhaps your voice was strong and clear, *Just as I am, without one plea* and *Pass me not, O gentle savior*. Whatever the boy thought, it did not keep him from calling. And when you married, he built a two-room log cabin on a section of your daddy's land, out in the middle of Laurel Fork Hollow. No, your flesh could not have repelled him, for he came to you, and came again, and together they filled their tiny cabin to bursting, him cutting trees while you cared for each of the babies that came, the days long, the nights short, everyone growing up fast, learning most of all to make do.

■ ■ ■

Some say sixteen, some say fewer. Thirteen babies are known to have survived. Thirteen satellites of the moon. Your children, Luna, and how you would have looked at their skin, first thing, just as your mama had done, scanning the whole of their bare bodies for signs of mottling. So much is unknown. Whether anyone came to help with the births. Whether your children's skin had the look of thin milk. What those babies thought as they grew, and looked into your face, whether they learned to think of all mamas as blue.

What is known is that they all grew into flesh as white as their father's. And so Luna, even in the company of your husband and your tribe of children, you remained one of a kind, leading a tribe of pale-skinned boys and girls into the woods to collect ramps in spring, frying them with potatoes and bacon fat, setting and clearing the table, until everything was set and you could rest a spell before rising to do it all again.

■ ■ ■

Blue. The feeling we have from time to time, so low, our hearts seem to have fallen into our shoes. The name given to the music freed slaves brought with them as they tramped north over the hills and hollows, songs as strong and slow as burnt molasses as they made its way into the sounds of the hills. Blue. Royal, cobalt, and turquoise. The color of queens and kings, and faraway seas. The color of eyes sometimes. Of berries and rivers and birds. Of certain bodies of water, of the sea, of the oceans—places heard of, but never seen.

■ ■ ■

But here I am once again making pretty your life, calling you a bird while talking up the hills of Eastern Kentucky, speaking of wild leeks and morning glories, conjuring the majesty of early morning. And there must have been that, of course, there must have been. But reality must interfere: mountainsides stripped of trees for logging, earth scraped for mining, hardscrabble days, the stretching of corn meal to feed fifteen mouths, buckets of water lugged from the creek, the cold of winter seeping into broken shoes, another baby to birth, another baby to bury, men using their bodies to cut chestnuts and poplars until their legs gave way like the trunks they cut into, the pennies becoming fewer, the mountain whiskey plentiful, the call of moonshine, the cry of the empty belly, clothes to wash and mend, the pile of things waiting for repair, the skins of men and women sagging from so much stooping.

■ ■ ■

So you were different. So there were flowers. So you lived in this world for eighty-four years. Was life ever more than was all those mouths to feed, squeezing into two rooms, sore bones and nowhere to stretch? Maybe skin color was the last thing to think about. Maybe it stopped mattering the moment you set yourself into motion. Still, it was another thing to carry, Luna. A special thing to be blue, perhaps, but when did it ever feel that way?

They cured the skin, you know. A doctor came traipsing through the hills with a needle, earning the trust of those few Fugates who still showed color, who let the doctor inject them and watched in wonder as their skin faded before their eyes. But that was after you, dear Luna, and for all of your days, you were blue.

And here I am a hundred years removed, and more than a hundred miles, but that doesn't stop my being drawn in by the strange color of you. How much I'd like to know you, to sit with you just once, to look into your face and see what shows beyond the skin. To hear your voice. To understand the world as you saw it.

What were the spaces like, Luna, those hours between the digging of potatoes and the mending of shoes? Were there times, when you stopped all that motion, set a hand upon knee, and looked up and into the trees. Times when it was just you and the dogwoods and whatever thing Jesus might have meant? *Just as I am, without one plea* and *Pass me not, O gentle savior.* Those old hymns, did you sing them to yourself? Did you meet the stares of others, head on, or go through life with your neck bent? No, somehow I know you lifted it high, your head, at least some of the times. And on those days, what did you think of the sky as you looked up and into its width—did it seem to you closer than kin, truer sometimes than the color of everything else? ■

RIGHT BEFORE THE WAKE

Charlie Fraley, I seen your face
first thing upon my passing
from this side to the next,
that devil's box shoved up
and underneath your chin,
sweat on your brow, all beaded
and dancing right along with the ductile
tune your bow eked out,
like silver in a jeweler's hands.

And there were leaves on the tree,
just out the window. I noticed
them while moving through
the streaked glass. The window
looking half melted with age,
and those leaves reached
out to wrap themselves around
my hands, and the branches
of that oak stretched
to run themselves through
my hair, just like my momma
used to with her knotty hands.

Charlie, you kept right on playing
while everything in sight kept time,
Lord, I can't blame them.
This was what I asked for,
my last hymnal, not a hymn at all.

All the while, that tree pulled me closer
to hollowed-out ground. I was done,
but that song, Charlie, I reckon it is still playing.

SAMANTHA LYNN COLE

A WORD ON REGRESSION

Hand reaching backwards through
time, and which was I? The murderer
or the murdered? Likely,
never a noble
dressed in lace,
not even a damn general.
A farmer, perhaps.
One who watched
the sun crane slowly across
the sky, creep from pole to pole,
who died with a spotted
face and shock-white hair.
Or a bum who killed
his wife when he found
her tucked away in some room
with another man, more sober,
laid the knife to her, red opening
like tulips. Just as easily, his woman,
spread on sheets stained with heartblood,
those figures later dulling
to the color of iron. It isn't, dear friends,
that I romanticize these things.
Such are marks of shame on the human head.
But, all-in-all, it is much more likely
than an Egyptian courtesan,
or the richest man in Prague.

SAMANTHA LYNN COLE

AN *APPALACHIAN HERITAGE* INTERVIEW

RICHARD HAGUE

Richard Hague is the thinker's poet, a masterful artist whose eight acclaimed poetry collections have grappled with physics and cosmology, the destruction of the Appalachian landscape, and his blue-collar upbringing in Ohio's Steel Valley. His book *During the Recent Extinctions: New and Selected Poems, 1984-2012,* received the 2012 Weatherford Award in Poetry, an annual prize presented by Berea College and the Appalachian Studies Association.

Over the years, Hague has shared his literary and creative knowledge in a variety of classrooms and settings, including the Appalachian Writers' Workshop, the Augusta Writers' Roundtable, and the Midwest Writers' Conference. For forty-five years, poet Richard Hague taught literature and writing at Purcell Marian High School, a Catholic institution in Cincinnati, where he was twice named Master Teacher by the faculty and designated the 2003 Teacher of the Year by the senior class. Earlier this year, Hague left Purcell Marian in protest, refusing to sign a new contract with the Archdiocese that expressly forbade a "homosexual lifestyle" as well as "public support" of one. His decision of conscience received national attention, including an article in the *New York Times*.

Hague chatted recently with *Appalachian Heritage* editor Jason Howard about his refusal to sign the contract, living a creative life, and his lengthy career as a poet and teacher.

■ ■ ■

JASON HOWARD: You grew up in Ohio's Steel Valley, working industrial jobs during summers for Wheeling Steel and Penn Central Railroad. How did that blue-collar background prepare you for life as a poet and creative writer?

RICHARD HAGUE: I'm not sure that it "prepared" me as a writer so much as it prepared me as a human being, coming slowly to an understanding of the great and often overwhelming power of industrial capitalism. My time in the work force then was utterly counter to today's world of small hand-held devices and desktop computers. I rode huge diesel locomotives and worked in the glare of open-hearth furnaces among men, mostly, who, if a Martian had observed them, would appear to have worshipped fire. If not fire, then football. There was a huge emphasis on physicality, on power, whether it was individual power exercised in the bluster and induced ecstasy of sport (or street fighting) or in working for steel mills, railroads, strip mines, power plants. The many subsidiary businesses—groceries, butcher shops, pharmacies, schools, healthcare agencies—really did not dominate or moderate the industrial capitalist culture; they served it… Everyone I knew was working class, or seemed it—even the professor at the College of Steubenville who attended my church and whose kids I went to school with. Work—of the industrial, mechanical kind, rather than an intellectual kind—was all we knew.

Despite this, though, I had a cadre of friends in high school who began to understand a larger world—I remember vividly first hearing Bob Dylan, in the tiny upstairs living room of my friend Roger Swartz, whose father operated a crane in the mill—and knowing, even almost saying the words to myself, *there is another world, one I have yet to see, and I will, I know I will.* [quotes Dylan's "The Lonesome Death of Hattie Carroll"] "William Zantzinger killed poor Hattie Carroll, with a cane that he swung on his diamond ring finger, in a Baltimore Hotel…"

Black people were mostly invisible in Steubenville in the mid-sixties; in twelve years of school I had been in class with maybe three. And the attitudes toward black people were generally benighted, to put it mildly. I learned all this on the streets and in the mills and on the railroad. But as with the case of Roger, and my buddy Charlie Joyce, and especially from girls I befriended and/or dated, the conversations became a bit more discerning. I would not say that by the time I left for college, I hated Steubenville, but it took me several

Richard Hague

years to understand its history and culture as a company town, then as an Appalachian town. (Part of this came as a result of my Master's thesis, a book of poems about the settlement and development and history of Steubenville—that helped me see it in a broader perspective). It was that education that prepared me as a writer. It was an education that went from uncritical but uncomfortable acceptance of a rather violent macho culture, through a questioning and rejection of that culture, to an understanding of the historical and economical and environmental cultural surroundings that allowed me to put it in some sort of perspective, and not simply to reject and hate it, but to experience it in its troubled and troubling complexity.

JH: Much of your poetry is grounded in the wild—it reminds me that Maurice Manning has called you a "naturalist" poet—and deals with the destruction of nature by heavy industry such as steel mills, chemical plants, and mountaintop removal mining. How did those topics begin to appear in your work?

RH: As my education in who I was and where I came from and how I was shaped by it all and how I maintained a difference from it all progressed, these things naturally became subject matter. Nature was a retreat for me; where others might have been fascinated by the possibilities of the T formation in football, or the chemistry of the Basic Oxygen Furnace, I was agog over the diversity in the sizes, colors, and habits of beetles...Also, my living in Monroe County, Ohio during several consecutive summers after college kept me in touch with nature, in a very rural environment. This was a great benefit to my writing—even though I hardly wrote at all during those summers, which I thought of as a vacation from writing and teaching. But I always returned at the beginning of fall ready to write again, and filled with subjects and details and characters.

JH: I read somewhere that you have called poems "living things." I love that—it's almost like thinking of them as an English oak or a creek. What do you mean by that term?

RH: My "teaching" book—which is also a collection of poems about poetry and writing, and an anthology of the best of my students' poems, and a handbook of prompts and writing tips, and a teaching memoir—is entitled *Lives Of The Poem*. The idea that poems are living things means that I have come to approach the writing of poems with a very submissive attitude—poems have a life of their own, separate and often counter to our "intentions" for them; learning to listen to what the poem wants to do has been the most fundamental lesson I've learned as a poet. It's different, a bit, for writing prose, but even then, I am alert to this one thing leading to that other thing, and that leading to something else, far beyond what I thought might happen when I began the essay or story. I hardly ever write a poem with a subject in mind; I just sit down and see what happens. Again, it's different for an essay or story, but serendipity is welcome always.

JH: Your most recent publication is *During the Recent Extinctions: New and Selected Poems 1984-2012*, **which won the 2012 Weatherford Award for Poetry. What made you decide to publish a volume of selected works at that point in time?**

RH: It seems that my first full-length collection, published in the ominous year of 1984 [with its] Orwellian implications and the wonderful year of 1984 [with] the birth of my first son, had started something: thus *Ripening*, its title. By 2012 my sons were grown, I was sixty-five years old, deep into the Anthropocene, increasingly aware of the endings of things (myself included). It simply seemed right to put those books that were really mostly nature poems or environmental poems together, and to let them, in their sequence, express a concern about the direction of things—increasing extinctions, climate change, the denaturing of American culture, and so on. Of course, there were other books than the ones collected in *During The Recent Extinctions,* and I was coming to realize then that there might be a second volume of selected poems, much more various, that did not 'fit" so well with the books in *Recent Extinctions*. So the second volume will be sequences and long poems, and its tentative and outrageously long title is *Beasts, River, Drunk Men, Garden, Burst & Light*. It's different, but some of the themes and issues are the same as in *Recent Extinctions*. So I selected the books of poems that best "fit" together for the first volume.

JH: I checked our archives, and you first published in *Appalachian Heritage* in 1979, a poem titled "Mr. Ealy Fishback" that used Chaucerian rhythms. What have you learned in all these years working at your craft?

RH: That I am not a "formalist" poet; I think there are less than a handful of my poems that rhyme, for example. It's not that I'm opposed to it, but I do feel deeply that a formalist writing philosophy arises from one of two sources: either a desire, conscious or even worse, unconscious, to control and order the world and its objects, or—and this is probably the same impulse—a belief that the world can always be made to "make sense." My lifetime of experience in both the human and natural realms simply does not allow for such a pat and orderly

Hague's most recent poetry collection, *During the Recent Extinctions: New and Selected Poems, 1984-2012,* won the 2012 Weatherford Award in Poetry.

vision. My most-often expressed conclusion about the majority of human affairs is that "reason does not prevail" and my most deeply intuited notions of nature suggest that much more mystery than clarity underlies everything: every beetle, mayfly, stone, river, or star is a book of infinite pages and connections.

Having said this, I readily agree that any art is a patterning, and that the patterning, to a greater or lesser degree, is a shaping, a forming. So any work of art is formal, in the broadest sense; pattern is also infinitely variable, and the pattern a poem may take (notice that the poem takes it; it is not so much imposed as discovered and submitted to) are also limited only by the scope of the human imagination. I don't need words falling into lockstep to thrill me when the vast possibilities, mysteriously coalescing on the page as I attend the poem, somehow solidify in so-called "free verse" into a new thing. That is a quiet, private, yet cosmic marvel.

Further, I am an ardent admirer of Shakespeare's sonnets, and they are among the most beautifully patterned works of art I know. I do not reject formalism; I suspect it in a modern, fragmented, disordered world; I reckon Shakespeare's attraction to form was his response to the chaos and uncertainty of Elizabethan England, with its Armadas, intrigues, executions, and explorations. It was also the fashion of the times as well. I am not resorting to formalist methods to defend myself against the world; I am letting the poem organize itself as it sees fit and as it can during these times.

I wrote "Ealy Fishbeck Knits Some Yarns On His Porch In Fly, Ohio" to get some laughs, to celebrate a fellow I'd met, and to poke some fun at city-slickers versus country wise men. Chaucer seemed a good model, especially the Chaucer of the General Prologue. Banging medieval England up against contemporary Appalachia seemed a funny thing to do, and I thought Al Stewart [celebrated poet and founding editor of *Appalachian Heritage*], whom I had become friends with at the Appalachian Writers' Workshop at Hindman, would enjoy it as well.

JH: What is the most important piece of writing advice you've ever received?

RH: Finish what you start. And after reading that fifty years ago (it's Hemingway), I'm still struggling to do it.

JH: You're well known for your generosity as a teacher, having taught at the Appalachian Writers' Workshop and various other creative writing conferences, as well as at Northeastern University in Boston and Purcell Marian High School in Cincinnati. How do you approach the classroom? What is your teaching philosophy?

RH: In a workshop setting, I constantly struggle with myself over excessive preparation on the one hand and improvisation on the other. Some of the best poems to come out of workshops I facilitate are those spinning off something that got said peripherally or some mis-hearing of something, or as the result of an argument that went far afield from the "topic at hand." I am a firm believer that in a workshop, all participants belong to one band of writers, and it is a band that shares everything; therefore, there is no such thing as 'stealing someone else's idea." Everything is up for grabs by every one. This creates diversity and excitement and opportunities and perhaps even a kind of *esprit de corps* that transcends individual "ownership." We're all in it together, and all "material" that rises out of our interactions is a commonwealth we all share, and spend.

In the subject matter classroom, "British Literature" for example, my practice was always mixed between lecture (after all, it's how I learn, too—trying to make sense of literature by talking and thinking out loud about it, with other minds in the room responding and questioning), and inquiry of one kind or another. But the biggest change in my teaching took place almost twenty years ago, and was based on my instinctive understanding, followed my own intense, conscious self-education in the subject, of what is called "constructivist learning." Briefly, it led me to give up control of the subject and assessment of learning, and to let the students take over and become responsible for their own learning, and, as far as possible, for their assessment of their own and each others' learning. This is a dangerous and exhilarating situation, and I do not recommend it to anyone but the most hardy and confident (and perhaps foolish) of teachers. Read Ted Sizer's triplet of books *Horace's School*, *Horace's Compromise*, and *Horace's Hope* and you'll see what I mean.

JH: You taught literature and writing at Purcell Marian, a Catholic high school, for forty-five years, where you were named Teacher of the Year and impacted the lives and work of many students. In May, in an act that generated national attention, you resigned that position and refused to sign a "morality clause," which prohibited teachers from "publicly supporting or engaging in a 'homosexual lifestyle,' sex outside marriage, artificial fertilization and other conduct that violates Catholic teaching," according to one news report. How did you arrive at your decision to resign?

RH: First of all, I did not resign. Resignation in much too passive a word for what I felt. I refused to sign the contract, I acted out a *non serviam,* as Stephen Dedalus does in *A Portrait of the Artist As A Young Man*. It is a useful and sometimes necessary position. After I first read the contract, I had a gut reaction to it; I found it arrogantly out of touch with the gentle, inclusive, welcoming side of Christianity, the side the school I worked in emphasized in word and deed. I had gay professors in college, I had gay colleagues at Purcell High School, I had gay students all through my career, I had and continue to have gay friends. To avoid "public support" of them, whatever that would be, seemed to me nothing short of betrayal—of them, of myself, of the long human evolution of friendship, of Christian principles, and not least of all, Catholic teaching on the primacy of individual conscience. I talked with dozens of people—priests, nuns, religion teachers, friends, writers—and was confirmed in my refusal to sign.

But it was not only this. The first line of the contract, its heading, reads "Teacher-Minister Contract." Suddenly, with no seminary training, no academic or spiritual counseling, and most certainly with no personal consultation with anyone at the Archdiocese, I was declared a "minister." This outraged me: it makes a part-time, non-Catholic soccer coach, say, as equally a "minister" as a religion teacher or a priest on the staff of a school. There is, to me, something vaguely blasphemous about this, as if anyone could be, without training, or divine calling, or without being struck from his horse on the way to Damascus, so to speak, a holy man or woman. And then I realized what it was all about: the 2012 Supreme Court decision called "the ministerial exception." The heading of the contract as "Teacher-Minister" is a way to dodge labor relations laws, anti-discrimination laws; it has nothing to do with spiritual matters, but is cold-bloodedly a legal maneuver to avoid liability under federal law. The Archdiocese had already been successfully sued for several violations of workers' rights and the dignity of workers; they seized on the Supreme Court decision to escape further payouts. And the burden of all this was, by this contract, transferred onto the backs of their employees. Disgraceful.

JH: I was so moved to read about the rally that was held on your behalf outside the Archdiocese in Cincinnati. One of your former students called you a "hero" and "mentor." Another stated, "One of my most talented teachers is stepping away from a job that he is a master at, years before he should." But you weren't even at the rally—you were in the classroom teaching and giving exams! How did that public support make you feel?

RH: Humble and a bit uncomfortable—I did not then nor do I now want to be the poster boy for this issue. I turned down many interviews with local and national press people at first. I was not intending to be the leader of some uprising, I was a private citizen, culturally Catholic if by then already excommunicated on several counts, and I saw this as an attack on individual conscience, as well as a ham-handed failure at dealing with a congregation which was losing members at a rate exceeding the numbers of Syrian refugees. How could they be so insensitive, so stupid? Nor could I forget a notion I'd discussed with generations of students who'd read "Letter From Birmingham Jail" and "On Civil Disobedience," a notion Dr. King termed "principled action." The term explains itself: you do as your heart and conscience tells you to do, not what others may think.

JH: Do policies like this shake your faith in the Church, or do you take hope in recent statements made by Pope Francis, who has spoken of a more inclusive Church?

RH: I think this contract was a response to Francis's much more inclusive tendencies, and to a possible liberalizing of Church attitudes on reproductive and marital issues, and a new focus on social justice. When the capitalists (who are behind the bishops just as surely as they are behind the other oligarchs in America) get a whiff of anti-capitalist sentiment, they go gaga. Or they write repressive and mean-spirited contracts.

JH: Do you believe that artists are particularly obligated to speak out against what they see as injustice?

RH: If the only "language" of resistance or critique were the language of "experts" trained in policy or law or governance, nobody would know what the hell was going on. One "Which Side Are You On?" is worth ten thousand words of acute political analysis. One *Guernica* is worth a library of arcane and academic critique.

JH: Many believe that one should keep art and politics separate, that issue-driven creative work could too easily turn into a polemic. Do you agree?

RH: Yes, issue-driven art can become polemical. This is something academics and aestheticians occasionally get exercised about. I don't care. If some social or institutional or governmental policy is wrong, it needs to be criticized. As Ted Sizer says in one of his great books about American high schools, a school (and a village and a neighborhood, and a state, and a nation) should be filled with judgments. Everything, every detail, should be up for judgment and discussion. However else can correction, and truth— and beauty—be realized?

If there were no great works of art that take a clear impassioned stand politically, then those who think art and politics should be kept separate are right. But see my previous answer, and, just for kicks, make your own personal list of great works of art [that] strike political points. Use them in your classroom, in your sermons, in your essays and blogs. They are some of the most potent and sharp tools of democracy.

JH: What are you working on at the moment?

RH: Keeping on this side of the grass, and finding peace. ■

FOUNDERED

A.W. MARSHALL

For the Wood family

"Someday you'll be dead and everyone else can eat," Iris said, after Floyd took the last of the mashed potatoes without asking if anyone wanted more. "Don't nod your head at me like that. I know what you're thinking."

"Shut up or I'll kick you into the living room," he replied.

We sat across from her grandparents at the kitchen table. Celeste and I had flown into Tulsa just two hours before.

"You. Just. Try it," Iris spit back.

And I smiled and wiped the sweat from my palms onto my jeans. I had already complimented the food a half dozen times, so I decided to not say that again. I came from a family who kept silent about their unhappiness until they couldn't take it anymore and then got really silent, like leave-the-state-and-don't-call-again silent.

It was early during dinner I realized Celeste had misled me about her grandparents. The only advice she gave me before entering was, "What they say means nothing. It's just their way." This was putting mildly what seemed destined for police tape. I couldn't understand how people allowed themselves to accept this "way." What way would Celeste and I become?

Celeste's grandparents raised her since she was four, her actual parents having disappeared, wasting their lives with drugs and selfishness. Twice during dinner her grandparents said Celeste was the best thing that ever happened to them. And God knows they were the closest and dearest people to Celeste's heart. When she moved to California to go to USC instead of the University of Oklahoma, both Celeste and Iris cried to each other on the phone for two weeks straight, one of them certain only the worst of things would come of it. Part of the purpose of this trip was to prove I wasn't one of those things.

When we drove up to their remote, single story house—long gravel driveway and white vinyl wrapped all around—I worried they wouldn't like me. When we entered, I realized my California childhood was far removed from this world. There was a roast on the table, surrounded by side dishes—baked beans, mashed potatoes, homemade gravy, fried okra, green beans cooked with bacon, raw onions, quartered tomatoes from the garden, and a plate of yeast rolls. So much I thought we'd never make a dent in it, but it turned out her grandfather knew something about eating my Californian upbringing couldn't comprehend.

As the food steadily disappeared, her grandmother kept apologizing for how the place looked, how her hair looked, how her husband looked, but to me it all looked like a real home. Every wall was wood paneled and nearly covered in photos of children, grandchildren, great-grandchildren and the long dead. The carpet was worn but clean. The kitchen table was cluttered and disorganized with catalogs and bills; a small TV flickered on mute. The living room table was brimming with carefully placed and dusted porcelain figurines—baby goats to Victorian ladies to winking gnomes with pipes.

After the mashed potato incident, Celeste decided to announce the reason behind our visit: we were getting married. Iris's approval of our marriage mattered most to Celeste because it was her grandmother's love and doting that had saved her when she was a child.

"So you kids are going to make a go of it," Iris said, "That's fine. I know Celeste loves you."

"Well, you don't say," Floyd said, gripping my hand in hearty handshake.

The whole thing seemed too easy. I would have sworn these two people would have immediate misgivings about marriage in general. But it was almost as if this wasn't a big decision, as if their granddaughter might not be on the precipice of ruin.

"If there's one thing I can count on," Floyd said, "Small fry knows what she's doing."

But Celeste didn't. I didn't. I proposed spontaneously and she accepted immediately. The next day we talked about it as if two other people were the ones who made this commitment. She wanted a career, to be free to see where it took her; I wanted to be safe, to be free to stay where I was. In general, we both just thought life was too uncertain, the future uncertain. What we might feel tomorrow, uncertain. Family was uncertain. The economy was uncertain. The president. Our own minds. Cars. Weather. Our hearts. All of it uncertain. So many people ended up with lives they didn't want. Neither of us understood how anyone could be sure. My father was a serial adulterer, my mother a lonely, hyperactive real-estate agent, my only sister a pill-popping elementary school teacher. Nobody was who they wanted to be. So many people drive

On the night I spontaneously proposed, Celeste and I got caught up in the moment, but afterwards we both knew the truth—we had probably made a mistake.

their lives into ditches. And I worried about what kind of even worse man I might turn into. On the night I spontaneously proposed, Celeste and I got caught up in the moment, but afterwards we both knew the truth—we had probably made a mistake. A mistake we couldn't see how to exactly undo as we did love each other. A mistake somehow binding and more comforting as we made it with the same skeptical frame of mind. Who better to share your life with than someone else that anticipated the worse?

So Celeste's grandparents took to me and our news with grace and kindness. In fact, both went out of their way to make me comfortable, to feel welcome. Iris knew I liked sweets and had two kinds of pies for me to choose from: blueberry and chocolate. After dinner, Floyd, a retired ironworker, gave me an elaborate tour of his shop, where he had made extra money welding anything metal to anything else metal since he retired twenty-five years ago. So I liked them both, if they were in different rooms.

As Celeste cleared the plates, her grandmother brewed some coffee. Her grandfather was beaming at his granddaughter, the family's only college graduate and his "small fry." While Celeste poured us all coffee and Iris cut pie, there seemed little left to say. Floyd started in with some old stories: about how his father chased some FBI men off his farm with a double-barreled shotgun when they came to slaughter some of his pigs for FDR's New Deal, about how he once cut his thumb off with an axe and his mother reattached it with turpentine and tape, how his father practically strangled Floyd's third grade principal when he found out the man was punishing his son by racking his hands with a yard stick.

"You hit his hands again and I'll kill you," Floyd's father apparently said. "A man makes a living with his hands. You beat his butt all you want."

I enjoyed the stories, but I could tell Iris was getting upset. She kept huffing and pulling her paper napkin into bits. I didn't know what was wrong, but it made me tense.

"If it's all right with you, I'd like to talk. You know other people like to say things, Floyd Wick," she said. "My mother also used turpentine on cuts," she told Celeste and me, "but there is no way you can put a finger back on with it. He's an old liar."

"It was my thumb! Right there," he said, holding it up for us to see, "There ain't much of a line there now. But that thumb came off and she put it back on. With turpentine. And tape. And you weren't there!"

"My ass," she replied. And all went quiet again.

"I've got to feed that dog," he grunted. He went to the closet for a jacket and slammed the sliding door on the way out.

"Mathew, do you need more pop?" Iris asked, smiling amiably, like this was all normal, like we could all get back to acting civilized now that the poo-throwing chimpanzee had left the room. "Maybe more pie. You hardly ate a bite at dinner."

I was bursting and begged off anything more.

"Celeste, go get him some more pop and pie."

"But he doesn't want anymore," Celeste pleaded.

On a dime, her grandmother's sweetness turned, "Nobody listens to me. Why can't I just ever be right?" Celeste reached over and rubbed her back.

When Floyd came back in, I admired his tan leather jacket. He had me touch it, very soft. He showed me how it was lined with sheep's wool and had a coyote fur collar.

"Manny Stark gave me this jacket," he said, "Gave it to me at least thirty-five years ago. You remember Manny, dummy?"

"Of course I do, I'm not addled, you fool," she said then turning to me. "Manny was a gentleman and a very kind man, unlike others."

"Came over one night and had a back seat full of jackets like this. Told me to pick any one I liked. A jacket like this cost a couple hundred dollars even then. Had to be around 1968."

"He was a gentleman," Iris said. "Very polite. And so good with cards. He could—"

"The man could hold any deck and—"

"I was telling it!" Iris yelled. She pursed her lips and squinted her eyes at him. I just sat there waiting, wondering if this was something or nothing. Was this serious or not? Then she turned to us. "You could ask for a Queen of hearts out of a deck of cards he'd never seen. He'd reach right in and pull it out. Did I say it all right, dummy?"

"Crooked as the day is long," Floyd said, ignoring her.

"Oh yes, his livelihood was crime. Not a villain, not bad, like some people. But an Oklahoma thief through and through."

"Until they kicked him out," Floyd added and she snorted, tired of being interrupted. "He had this truck with this flat bed trailer on it, a big ol' jack welded to the end. He'd pull up to any business he wanted on a Sunday and jack up their loading dock door. Drag anything he could on the trailer. Every time I saw the man he had something."

"His wife was Estelle," Iris broke in, "a hard woman to know. Kind of curt. But we used to all get together and play cards for pennies until one or—"

"He'd throw whatever it was on the trailer—refrigerators, boxes of soap, beer, whatever, and have it sold by nightfall and go home to the family. He was—"

I was sure someone was going to get up and find a knife. But Celeste just sat there, looking down in her lap. If she could put up with these people, I would be a piece of cake.

"We were good friends! All of us, good friends!" Iris yelled, cutting him off. She turned to Celeste and me, a sudden, sweet gentleness shining through. "So Estelle and I would lay out some chips, maybe some nice dip. A pickle platter. Cold cuts for sandwiches with some nice—"

"One time," Floyd said, and Iris slammed her hand on the table. They stared at each other, and I looked at Celeste for help. I was sure someone was going to get up and find a knife. But Celeste just sat there, looking down into her lap. If she could put up with these people, I would be a piece of cake.

"One time he gave me a .357 magnum," Floyd started up again. "Brand new. A beaut. Nickel with rosewood grips. That Estelle came and got it one day. Demanded it back."

"She needed the money, you runt. She needed that gun to buy food for those kids." Iris turned to us to explain, "Manny was told to leave Oklahoma and never come back. Estelle stayed because her family was here. Can't follow a wild man like that. Some just aren't made for family life. Both Estelle and I drew duds."

"Manny gave me that gun," Floyd explained to me, "but I gave it to her. He was a friend, after all."

"You made it hard enough for her to get it, didn't you? She had to sit at this very kitchen table while you hemmed and hawed for an hour. Poor thing was embarrassed enough already."

She stared at him, daring him to deny it, rubbing it in that he was crummy to someone thirty years ago. I looked at Celeste who attempted to smile at me. Her eyes said, "They're crazy but they raised me and I'm sorry you have to sit through this." My eyes said, "No wonder you were worried about getting married."

"One time Manny came over," her grandfather said, directing this right to me and Celeste, making it clear this story was for us only, despite whoever else might be in the room. "And he asked me a favor. He had seventeen stolen TV sets and he was going to trade them for seven horses. He needed a trailer and wanted to see if I could help. This was before I built that shop and had all those ol' junkers back there."

Suddenly, Celeste's grandmother stood up and stomped out of the room, toward the restroom. Celeste watched her go. Then she reached for my hand, I'm not sure why. She smiled when I looked over. I tried to imagine calling her "dummy" or saying "I'll kick you in the head," but I just couldn't. But Floyd and Iris probably never imagined saying such things either. When they were first married they probably held hands and talked in the dark.

"So, I borrowed a large open trailer and we headed down to the blackjacks," Floyd continued. "Most pathetic place to live you ever seen. We carried those TVs into this clapboard shack and the man led us out back. 'Manny,' I say, 'these horses are wild.' See he didn't know about horses. Wild horses are more trouble than they are worth. I explained to him how they were never ridden, never saddled, and probably mean as sin after being corralled like this. Well, he went and talked to the man, and they must have come to some sort of agreement because he said, 'Let's load 'em up, Floyd.'"

We heard Iris talking to herself in the bathroom. We stopped and listened, and all I could make out was "big fat stupid liar." She was telling him off. He shook his head and kept on.

"By hook or by crook, we load these horses on the trailer. They didn't want to go and it took some whipping. The moon was in the wrong place so it was dark like a gypsy. These ol' horses hustling about, and me with a flashlight and a whip. See, if I knew they were wild I wouldn't have borrowed this trailer. It had no roof and the sides came to just below their shoulders. By the time we were on the highway, they were in panic. Whinnying and kicking each other. Then a chestnut mare with a black mane jumped and its front legs went over the side. That was big trouble."

Iris came back in and cut me another slice of pie. Her face was washed and her eyes were puffy. She poured herself a pop, ignoring Floyd's empty glass.

"I knew if that horse leapt out we'd have trouble. If we stopped the truck, all the panicked horses would have jumped out of the trailer and been all over the highway. And to truck on and leave that dead horse on the road would probably kill someone if they weren't paying attention, and most people don't. So I hit the brakes and that ol' horse flopped back in. We got to the house and unloaded the horses back there with the horses I got for the kids."

"Liar," Iris said. "Those horses were yours. Kids were lucky to pet 'em."

His face steamed into red. His work-worn hands curled into giant lumps. How do people turn out like this? I wondered. What do they neglect or let happen that leads to this? I had this urgent desire to see them at breakfast on some regular morning, just the two of them, to see them in their natural habitat—to see if they made nice.

Floyd gritted his teeth and kept on, "Manny asks if I can break 'em. I tell him I can. I explain it will take over a month. I was working, you see. Anyway, he says that's all right. No talk of money."

"If you can believe that," Iris looked at me, nodding, trying to communicate that if her husband has convinced me of one single, noble thought on his behalf I should get rid of it. "This man would kick a dying dog for a dollar." I laughed like she made a joke and Celeste did too, and so did he, but bitterly. Celeste patted her grandmother's hand, and Iris looked at the two of us, then smiled, cordially enough. Then she turned to me.

"I'm going to get you some milk for that pie, Mathew." She had stopped asking me if I wanted more food or more to drink and was simply daring me not to consume what she put in front of me.

"Anyway," Floyd said, "the next day I go out back and see some of the horses have foundered. The pen was flecked with blood and a few of them horses were walking on their knees. Sweating, all their muscles trembling. A pathetic sight. That man probably gave those wild horses all the grain and water they wanted and ruined their intestines. Nothing Manny could do with foundered horses. I called him and said he needed to get these horses out of here. He didn't know what to do so I called a man I knew and he said they would buy the horses for dog food."

"You should have seen it," Iris said, "A horrible sight. All those horses, wild as God made them, destroyed by greedy, cruel, selfish men." Then she pointed right at Floyd.

"What could I do, honey? You know how much it would have cost to treat them?"

"If you had it, you still wouldn't have done it! Hell, if you thought horse was fit to eat, you would have tried to make me cook one that same night. You've always treated me like a dog anyway. But I wouldn't have! I would not have cooked that horse!"

We all stared at her. I suppose we wanted to understand what exact statement she was trying to make—against him, against mankind. For herself. What was she so desperate to claim about herself? Then Celeste burst out laughing. Iris looked at her and started to chuckle.

"Well, you know," she said, "I wouldn't have."

"So the man came out," Floyd drove on, directly to me now, undeterred by any of it. "By that time most were a mess to look at. A few had their front legs pushed out in front of them, their back legs buckling with the new pressure. They'd fall over and struggle to get back up. The man said we'd have to move fast. That once they fell we'd be in for some ugly work. God, we had to whip those horses raw to get 'em onto the trailer. My horses were spooked. One kicked and broke a foundered horse's rib. Cracked like a bullet going off. The foundered horses' knees were bloodied from crawling up the metal ramp. Every darn one screaming and crying. But one horse, that chestnut mare, wouldn't go. We whipped and whipped her and she wouldn't budge. She snarled and snapped her teeth at us. Poor wild thing. But I knew if she didn't go then I'd be stuck with a dead horse. I asked the man, 'Does it matter what condition this horse is in when it gets in the trailer?' 'It don't,' he said."

I flinched at what might come next, my imagination conjuring a cruelty I would not be able to smile through. Floyd didn't quite realize how awful his story was. He thought he was telling us about how Manny's deal went sour. No worse than explaining how to change a tire. He didn't realize he was talking about how some wild horses were trapped and killed for nothing. I tried to crawl into his mind. Tried to see how he saw the horses. How he saw life. But I couldn't.

"So I called Ol' Buck. Buck was our Australian Shepherd. Best family dog ever. And tough as nails," he said.

"No man could touch that gate without Buck making it clear he'd kill him if he came through," Iris said, proudly. "A fine family dog."

I tried to crawl into his mind. Tried to see how he saw the horses. How he saw life. But I couldn't.

I heard a sniffle and saw Floyd was tearing up, "One day he was out front and a neighbor saw a man purposely swerve off the road to hit Buck. What for? Why do such a thing? Killed him on the spot. The only reason he was out there was the school bus was due to show up and he liked to meet the kids."

"How would you know? You were at work. It was around noon, you old fool. And it was summer! The kids were playing out back in the kiddie pool. Who knows why Buck was out there, but a school bus had nothing to do with it."

"By shit, you better leave me be," Floyd said, rubbing his cheeks dry.

"If only things happened like you make them up."

Then she turned towards Celeste and me. She must have seen the expression on my face. I can't remember what I was thinking, but it stopped her for a second.

"You don't know what I've put up with," she said. "Day in and day out. This is just today. Married him at fourteen. What did I know? I only knew what I hoped for. I needed get away from my father, but I had dreams. Maybe a little store to sell nice things. Some china, Wedgewood. Things ladies like. Take some trips—Europe, Hawaii, places. I had a future in mind for myself. So many things in mind, gone now. Instead yelling, drinking, and, yes, violence, don't let him fool you. Such cruelty he had in mind for me. How was I to know what marriage could be? Gone forever. You never know what life can be when you're young."

Celeste was crying, but I knew it was also because of the horses and Buck. About us. Her grandparents. Just the whole lot of it together. All to hear about a man no one had seen in thirty years. And I knew she was worried about me, about the impression I was getting and it was probably dawning on her, like it was me, that this was the first night of a five-day visit.

"What's wrong dear?" Iris asked, suddenly concerned. Her face turned into tender mercy, and I could see all the love she had for Celeste. Floyd reached across and held Celeste's hand. "Did grandpa make you upset? I'm sorry. I really am. Don't you pay us no mind."

"We're just two old, stupid people," Iris said.

"It's just been a long day, that's all," Celeste said.

"Nothing could be done for those horses, small fry," Floyd continued. "That dumb man in the blackjacks did it. It's a horses' life that happened to them. I was sorry they had to suffer like that. It wasn't right."

"It's okay, Grandpa."

He coughed. His hand still resting on hers.

"Well, I better finish this story," Floyd continued, watching Celeste carefully, "Like I was saying, I had to get that horse in the trailer. So I called Ol' Buck over. And I said, 'git that horse!' And by god, he knew exactly what I meant. He tore after that horse and didn't even have to take a chunk out. The horse saw Ol' Buck coming and wobbled and crawled into the trailer lickety split. Man gave Manny $125 for all that meat. Worse deal he ever made. And I didn't see a nickel for all my trouble."

"But you got your precious jacket and your precious gun."

"I gave the gun back!"

"What a generous heart you have," Iris said.

"What happened to Manny?" I asked, trying to cut them off.

"Well, like we said," Floyd answered, "Oklahoma police told him to git and never come back and he didn't. See he stole a shotgun out of a police car. God knows what became of him after that. He was wild and couldn't work an honest job."

"He was adopted," Iris added. "To a good family too. And he turned out like that. Who would have guessed? Makes you wonder who his real people were."

I took out my phone. I asked them to spell his name. Celeste told them what I was doing and they said he had to be dead and buried by now, and I certainly wouldn't find him on any phone.

"What happened to Estelle?" Celeste asked. Her face sparkled with drying tears.

"Poor baby," Iris said, patting Celeste's hand. "Well, let's see. Estelle took up with a man named Tom. Tom was a drunk and a creep and she got rid of him. And now she lives alone, just a few blocks from here."

"Place is a shame to look at," Floyd said, "Least her son could do is mow the lawn."

"But I've never heard you talk about her. Are you still friends?" Celeste asked.

"I suppose we just lost touch. She was a hard woman," Iris said.

Apparently Manny did come back to the state. Oklahoma Department of Corrections had three photos. Manny was arrested for meth manufacturing in 1993 and then in 1996, when he was sixty-two. The third photo was just a few months before he died of cancer while incarcerated. I showed them the photos, and they just couldn't stop looking.

"He looks so old," Iris said, "He used to be a nice looking man."

"I'd never have guessed drugs," Floyd said. "What a good for nothing."

But there was more. Things they didn't know to recognize. The small scabs on his face. The space between his teeth from where his gums receded. The loss of weight. The mean hunger in his eyes. How his face wasn't just old, but blanched and haggard, used, heavy with fatigue. All the classic signs of serious meth use. I imagined the hopes and dreams his adoptive parents had when he was a baby, how they thought they were giving him a better life. How as he grew into a child, he began to believe in those dreams too. Until what.

I imagined the hopes and dreams his adoptive parents had when he was a baby, how they thought they were giving him a better life.

After her grandparents went to bed, I moved into Celeste's old bedroom while she washed her face. I looked up what foundered meant on my phone and read about how stress creates acid which eats at the complex carbohydrates in the grain creating a serious inflammation, particularly in the lower joints, which is why the horses fell. Floyd's story was a worst case scenario, but even if that didn't happen, even if Manny made money, that wouldn't have made any of it a bit better. What Floyd couldn't understand was that his story was about lovely, pure, wild things destroyed by poor intentions turning to crap.

Celeste came in, her face bright and clean, but her eyes were tired. We didn't say anything as we unpacked and arranged our stuff. Then she sat on the edge of the bed, rubbing lotion into her face and hands; I lay on my back staring at the popcorn ceiling. The night, I suppose, was noisy enough. After we turned off the lights and moved into her old bed, Celeste started to cry.

"What's wrong, sweetheart?" I asked.

"I don't know. I'm sorry about tonight."

"It's okay. It wasn't that bad."

She chuckled. She shifted her body and I felt her head tuck up under my chin, her lips breathing against my neck. I pulled her close.

"You were very sweet," she said, and her lips kissed behind my ear. "Sometimes I wonder what's the use."

"I know," I said.

She lifted her head. Her tongue was warm and salty. I dragged my foot down her calve.

"What are we going to do?" she asked.

I kissed her nose. Her forehead. She slid down her pajamas. Everything was so quiet as her fingers hooked around my shoulder blades. I rolled on top of her.

"We'll get married," I breathed into her neck.

"Will we have kids?"

"Yes," I said. "We'll make babies. Tons of them." She giggled, but I could almost see it. Not minding it. The promises. The hopes. The plans. What it could all end up like.

"Okay," she said.

■ ■ ■

The next day, I helped Floyd load some old metal onto his flatbed to sell for scrap. He gave me gloves, but didn't put any on himself when he started grabbing into the sharp and rusty metal. He was seventy-eight, and he still looked like he could tear me up. Though he groaned and exclaimed, he threw things I had trouble lifting. I don't think I was much help but he seemed to really appreciate the attempt. He told me more stories: injuries on the job, kids and Christmases, the Korean War—"All those good, young men killed across the world."

But what I wanted to know about was him and Iris. I wanted to understand what made them settle down together. And what made them stay. How did things end up like that? Did they ever get along? At night, when no one was there, did they hold each other? Did they talk in the dark? But I didn't have the guts, so I asked about Manny. I asked if he seemed to like being a criminal.

"I don't know," he said. "I think it was maybe not wanting a regular job. And he lost his family cause of it. And look how he ended up. No, I just think he was lazy and because of that his life ended up lousy."

Later, while we drove the bed full of metal to the scrap yard, I thought about the horses on that trailer, saw myself among them, how we bucked against each other, whinnied in terror. Our only home growing small behind. Wondering where the open plains and quiet disappeared to. The chestnut horse's legs thrown over the rail. Eyes bulging. Asphalt screaming underneath. Metal to hoof shocking up our legs, the grain and water heavy in our bellies—all the new, treacherous things. Our legs twisting to the ground the next morning. The red lights backing up. The explosion as the tailgate dropped. The loud whooping and hollering from the men. Lastly, the tight metal pen, the gun up to my head.

"Don't tell that one inside the house this," Floyd said as we pulled out of the junkyard, "but Manny was no gentleman either. He ran around on Estelle anytime he could. It was a different kind of stealing to him. He acted like a good husband, played the role—charmed Iris every time he was over—but he chased tail all day long. Just goes to show, only one thing is sure, you just never can tell nothing about nothing." ■

MIDSUMMER

Under the old redbud in the boulevard,
sound umbrellas our heads, lifted as to thunder.
Near oh near, they cry above us, and together,
though deaf in their midst, we speak the names
we have learned in lives brief and long. *Cicada,*
says my granddaughter, given by her mother.
Jarflies, I counter, word my grandmother broke
with half-runners on newsprint spread in our laps,
far, so far on that glider, that porch, those burnished
evenings. In the dying down, the four-year-old
affirms the stamp of science: *ci-ca-da,* not yet
surefooted in the gloaming, the papers we'll flatten
with corn shucks, oilcan she'll fetch for our rocking
to and fro. In the new ringing, like all deepness
wrung from pitched joy, we look and look
for the red eyes, the jewel wings, near,
oh near in the shattered still-lit night.

LINDA PARSONS MARION

THIS SHAKY EARTH

An overly sensitive heart is an unhappy possession on this shaky earth—Goethe

I've run out of verbs on the shoulder of I-75.
Semis barrel, no, blast, no, *thunder* past
my blown-out Outback, the shimmy I ignored
for thirst of home, tire that looked fine
at my aunt's in Georgia, stranding me south
of Chattanooga, as my mother would say,
flat as a flitter.

In the moment a trucker glances toward
the pine ridge, I would stop waiting for AAA
without a cup to pee in, stop thinking
of the street preacher's exhortations: *Repent,*
ye wastrel, the end is at hand. In that brilliance
between here and yon, I would have no knowledge
of hosta unfurled or sweet singe of Pepsi,
no more flutter in the chest, my husband's
salt skin. I would be what remains of blithe
inattention, grease darkening the asphalt,
the earth barely shaken.

After my aunt's arrhythmia, the impulses
checked by ablation, we sat in her kitchen,
around us her flow-blue china, the years
she cared for a husband with MS, his spasms
dirtying the sheets. Familiar though lapsed,
we called for rescue and recovery,
our murmurs half-drowned in the arteries
of traffic and waste. *Be still, my heart,*

we called, both needing to be shocked
from time to time on the side
of the treacherous road.

LINDA PARSONS MARION

LIVING
IN THE RIVER OF WORDS:
Rejection and Acceptance

GEORGE ELLA LYON

Recently I was asked to talk about the experience of having one's work rejected, so I began by listing highlights of such low points in my own writing life.

- The one from the high school teacher who said I couldn't have written the poem I turned in so I must have plagiarized it.

- The one that got blown from the mailbox and frozen in the forsythia bush.
- The one that said "these poems appear to be held together with snot." (I checked. They weren't.)
- The one that said "we like your work but the past is a fad."
- And the one which turned down a villanelle, a poem with recurring lines, for being repetitious.
- The one which cited "no coherent underlying voice."
- The one which arrived via cell phone right before I was to give a talk.
- The one which called my memoir "too reflective and self-aware."
- The one which said "cut the writing."
- The one which said "the second draft isn't as powerful as the first; the characters don't have enough of an arc."
- The one that said the novel didn't work; then, when I asked how to revise it, the editor said, "Please don't."
- The one where the editor asked what I thought the manuscript's weak spots were and, after I identified them, said, "Exactly! That's why I'm rejecting it."
- The ones I got for poetry manuscripts for the first eleven years I sent books out.
- The one where the editor called to make sure I got the rejection.
- The ones that arrive via inbox, mailbox, iPhone for eighty percent of everything I send out.
- The ones I give myself.

So how does a person keep going amid the rejections that are guaranteed to come with the territory? Well, there are also acceptances.

- The time someone sang in my dream and I woke up and wrote the rest of the song.
- The time a character's voice was so strong I felt like I was writing to uncover words that were already on the page.
- The first time I was paid enough for a reading that I was able to put gas in the car.
- The times when my writers' group cheers.
- The time I was so deep in writing that joy woke me up early and got me to the page.
- The time a child slept with my book under her pillow
- The time I was working on a shape poem which my computer couldn't handle, so I printed the words in a standard format, then cut them out to paste on the page the way I wanted them. Then came the moment when all my fingertips had words stuck to them and laughter rocked me like the ocean between waves.
- The shower-of-shivers moment when I realize that a piece I'm working on has something I couldn't give it, and I feel I'm living in the mystery.
- The time my editor asked if I needed money and, when I said yes, gave me an advance for a book that didn't exist yet. He suggested we call it *Charade*.
- The time someone sent an email which said, "Your poem made us cry, so now we're going to have a party."
- The embrace when someone tells me a part of their story because of something I've written from mine.
- The moments when writing is flowing in such a way that the page or the screen themselves seem to be helping; when I feel so supported by what is moving through me that it carries me beyond acceptance and rejection into joy and revelation.

But how do you get from rejection to acceptance, from feeling outside the great conversation of writing to being immersed in it?

First, it's crucial to understand that the moments of acceptance are just that, moments. They're not a place you go live. But the same holds true for rejections. They're *moments*, not proclamations about the worth of your words or of your future as a writer. Rejections mean you're doing your work and sending it out.

So what do you do in between those rare moments of acceptance to save you from the dejection that the all-too-frequent rejections can create? You WRITE. You establish a practice for writing. You find your joy in the process, which is the one place you can count on it.

You will find your own metaphor for it, but I call this practice Living in the River of Words.

I liken this to learning another language. The most effective and efficient way to do that is to enroll in an immersion program, preferably in a country where the language is spoken. If that's not possible, the school becomes its own little country where you study, read, speak, eat and dream in your new tongue. You are persistently drenched in French, German, Russian, Arabic—whatever you signed up for—and, just as when you were little and learning your first speech, your brain has to have a festival of synapse-making. You learn because you have to be able to request food, ask questions, find the bathroom. Necessity is the mother of attention.

Now imagine something similar as a writer, only it's your own language you are learning. Your own voice fed by the mythic sea of the unconscious, the myriad rivers of literature, the everflowing wellspring of language itself. If you submerge yourself in this source, really give yourself over to it regularly, you will be amazed at what happens.

Many writers use the metaphor of the river when they talk about process:

Jim Haba, poet and editor of Bill Moyers's *The Language of Life*, speaks of "the anonymous river of poetry."[1]

William Stafford says:

> *Writing is peculiarly susceptible to this wonderful resource, language. I didn't invent it, I don't control it. It just rolls on. It comes from everybody. It's not something I learned from other writers, by any means. It's not something I learned from critics, by any means. It is a great river of possibilities swirling around us all the time. People talk to each other and come upon—I guess I do it like a gull—these great swoops of realization and vistas that veer off toward other formulations in language. And even the syllables have meaning.*[2]

Remember Stafford's words: "I didn't invent it. I don't control it." This is a key principle of the river, because like all art—all life—writing is about discipline and surrender. It takes discipline to wade into that river again and again, farther and farther, until you become available to its flow, its power focused by your intent or the intent of whatever is working through you at the moment. If you try to take too much credit or to build locks and dams, your agenda pulls you out of the river and you soon find yourself high and dry. I have done this often enough to know.

1 Bill Moyers, *The Language of Life: A Festival of Poets*, ed. James Haba (New York: Anchor, 1996), 285.

2 Ibid., 96.

Essential to living in the river is getting over the idea that art is something we do to create a product. Art is a process of collaboration between us, our material, and the river, which includes our tradition. We engage in the process—whether as creators or as audience—to get in touch with our souls, another principle of the river.

Former Poet Laureate Rita Dove says, "I would like to remind people that we HAVE an interior life—even if we often don't talk about it because it's not expedient, because it's not cool, because it's potentially embarrassing—and without that interior life, we are shells, we are nothing."[3]

Dutch writer and priest Henri Nouwen puts this in river terms: "When the deepest currents of our life no longer have any influence on the waves at the surface, then our vitality will eventually ebb, and we will end up listless and bored even when we are busy."[4]

Writing is a collaborative process by which we get to those deep currents, discover our interior life and bring it forth. "Bringing it forth" is another principle.

What do I mean by collaboration? Four things. First, there is a spirit that wants something new to happen. It is in you but it is not you; you are part of it. It is, as Dylan Thomas wrote, "the force which through the green fuse drives the flower."[5] It wants you to bloom, too, to share your essence with the world. As Gerard Manley Hopkins put it in "As kingfishers catch fire":

Each mortal thing does one thing and the same:
Deals out that being indoors each one dwells;
Selves—goes itself, myself it speaks and spells,
Crying, What I do is me: for that I came.[6]

You are not alone in your impulse to create, to say something. You are supported by your nature and the nature of the universe. What moves Creation moves you.

The second collaborator is your medium, that river of language itself. It includes all the richness of English and any other languages in your acquaintance, all the voices your grew up with, all the literature—and everything else—you've read, all the words that come at you daily via every manner of screen plus our conversations and our dreams. It is the magic of rubbing any two words together. Cosmic toes, for example. Briney hillocks. Shredded Internet.

Third, the river is your unconscious: what you dream, the parts of yourself you reject—your Shadow, Jung calls it—your

We don't just put words on the page and push them around. We listen to them, let them lead us.

ancestors' voices, genetic memory, our collective unconscious. I like to think of it as a story table, like the water table, that flows underneath everything, and which we can reach when we go through our deepest selves and then deeper, into the energy beyond us. All of this is available if we make ourselves available to it.

Finally, we collaborate with the thing we are making. We don't just put words on the page and push them around. We listen to them, let them lead us. We not only revise our writing, we let ourselves be revised. Indeed, this is why the process can take so long. Changing words is one thing. Changing a human being is another.

3 Ibid., 125.

4 Henri J.M. Nouwen, *Life of the Beloved: Spiritual Living in a Secular World* (New York: The Crossroad Publishing Company, 1992),

5 Dylan Thomas, "The force which through the green fuse drives the flower" in *The Poems of Dylan Thomas* (New York: New Directions, 2003), 90.

6 Gerard Manley Hopkins, "As kingfishers catch fire" in *Gerard Manley Hopkins: The Major Works* (Oxford: Oxford University Press, 2009), 129.

In *Art & Fear*, an enormously helpful look at the creative process by David Bayles and Ted Orland, the authors declare: "Art happens between you and something—a subject, an idea, a technique—and both you and that something need to be free to move."[7]

Free to move—a wonderful, essential phrase. Imagine trying to stand, unmoving in a river. What would happen? Maybe you could do it for a while, confining your vision to that one place, but eventually your resistance would be overcome, and if you kept fighting the flow, kept trying to keep yourself out of the river even while you were in it, you would wear yourself out. You might swim to shore; you might go under and be lost.

Of course, you can also just wade, keeping close to the bank, not really in, not really out. Dabbling, we call it. And you may write some pretty things, some clever things, some witty, smart, or caustic things. But you will not write from your center, where your powerful voice is. As the proverb goes, "If you wish to drown, do not torture yourself with shallow water."

Wait a minute, you say. I didn't sign on for drowning! Me neither. But as poet Lucille Clifton says, "You cannot play for safety and make art."[8] And, scary as it may be, drowning in the river of words is like dying in a dream. It's a good thing. It means you've let go of something that needed to go. As the Brier exhorts us in Jim Wayne Miller's "Brier Sermon," "You must be born again!" And you don't get reborn without . . . guess what? Dying to the old self, the self that held itself apart, that thought you were alone and in charge.

Another principle of the river: you are not alone. All the riches of language are with you, all you have read and heard, all in the unconscious—personal and collective—and all you can learn from the words that are coming to you. I return to Bayles and Orland in *Art & Fear*:

The work we make, even if unnoticed and undesired by the world, vibrates in perfect harmony to everything we put into it—or withhold from it. In the outside world there may be no reaction to what we do; in our artwork there is nothing but reaction.

The breathtakingly wonderful thing about this reaction is its truthfulness. Look at your work and it tells you how it is when you hold back or when you embrace. When you are lazy, your art is lazy; when you hold back, it holds back; when you hesitate, it stand there staring, hands in its pockets. But when you commit, it comes on like blazes.[9]

But how do you do this? In *A Poetry Handbook*, Mary Oliver says:

[O]ne can rise early in the morning and have time to write (or, even, to take a walk and then write) before the world's work schedule begins. Also . . . one can live simply and honorably on just about enough money to keep a chicken alive. And do so cheerfully.
This I have always known—that if I did not live my life immersed in the one activity which suits me, and which also, to tell the truth, keeps

7 David Bayles & Ted Orland, *Art & Fear: Observations on the Perils (and Rewards) of Artmaking* (Eugene: Image Continuum Press, 2001), 20.

8 Moyers, 91.

9 Bayles & Orland, 49.

me utterly happy and intrigued, I would come someday to bitter and mortal regret.[10]

There is no prescription for living in the river, but here are some suggestions: list it among your day's necessities. Work, grocery, bank, laundry, river. Or river first, if possible, if you're an early riser. But river has to be on the list of priorities. It is how and where your spirit is renewed. It is how you are you. Plan on it, like exercise. We all know exercise doesn't just happen. Sitting in front of reruns eating Bugles happens. Endless email happens. Surfing the web and missing the river.

Everybody's days are different, their structure dictated in some measure by jobs, family, and community. The river runs under all of them. It may seem that because I'm a freelance worker, getting to the river is easy for me. I can plunge into it in my pajamas. Well, sometimes I can and I do. But other times, I get to where I think the river was and it feels like the Sahara. Or I can see the river but a tree has fallen across the path. Or I put my hand in the river and it's nothing but silk scarves. What do I do then?

First, I try the old trick of writing about not being able to write. I get my journal or I open a file called "Self-Direction" and I talk to myself about what's in the way. I ask myself what I'm afraid of, what I'm distracted by, what I'm not saying. Sometimes this causes that tree to slide on down the mountain or those scarves to wave themselves back into water. Sometimes it doesn't, so I make more coffee. If coffee doesn't help, I read. If I have a book I'm studying on my desk, I read that. If another writer's work calls me, I turn to those words. I wade into that river. Many times someone else's words will send me right back to the page.

If that fails, I sing.

If singing doesn't do it, I take a walk. Just moving around outside can lift me over the stuck place.

If that doesn't work, I go have the oil changed in the car or wash the bathroom ceiling or do whatever task is pulling at the space between my ears and holding me out of the river. But I aim to set a time limit on this interruption.

Since I can't make my living from books, there are many days when I have other jobs. And jobs bleed into the writing time, because I can't give talks without writing them or do workshops without preparing for them. I've seen both done, and the results are unfortunate. Besides time spent at the job itself, there's time preparing, packing, and driving.

But river has to be on the list of priorities. It is how and where your spirit is renewed.

Nobody pays me for this time. Or rather, the honorarium I'll receive is for all of it. It also has to help support the work for which I never get paid, which is most of what I write. I have an average of fifty-five jobs a year. Some require a day, some a week. Most I drive to, some I fly. I've spoken in elegant hotels and in bowling alleys and petting zoos. (Do not try that last venue! Nothing you can read is as interesting as a llama kids can touch.) The audiences range from writers and teachers to directors of college social work programs, to elementary students wearing Indian costumes made out of grocery bags and fluorescent feathers. Two summers ago I found myself in an old theater yelling through a megaphone to 150 kids dressed as pirates ...

The point is that I have to navigate the territory between the pirates and the river. I have to go from a teaching situation,

10 Mary Oliver, *A Poetry Handbook* (Boston: Mariner Books, 1994), 120.

however bizarre, in which I more or less know what I'm doing, to writing, where all my knowing only gets in the way.

Stanley Kunitz says "the first important act of the imagination is to create the person who writes the poems."[11] You create that person by your steadfast devotion, by your practice. You accept yourself and the fact that you must surrender to the uncertainties, the mystery of artistic work. This is how you honor your gift. This is how you pass it on. ■

11 Moyers, 244.

SOUTH

Even the ground feels aggrieved, steeped
in the death spittle of Confederate greys,
tears of miners' brides, spilt shine
from a last run with the law. Bloodlines,
family names—they haunt, fix you, accuse:
Hatcher, Raper, Boring, Joines. Misery,
salvation, damnation, the Appalachian
sublime—cardinal points, no means of escape.

RICHARD E. JOINES

QUEEN

LEAH HAMPTON

In her memory, the hive sat in the side yard, echoing family rituals and routines. Summer mornings, workers would swarm the basil plant on the porch. They bothered no one—not even Dale, whose deck chair always sat close by.

Maisy could scarcely think of when she had ever been stung on her mother's property. So familiar were the movements and flight paths of all participants that it never occurred to anyone to disturb each other. The spread of acres kept them all satisfied to amble their own way, and making room for others rarely interrupted anyone's foraging. So when Dale texted her about the half empty hive and the carnage littering the hydrangea bushes, Maisy left work early, pulled her hair up into a ponytail, and barreled down Highway 23 to her mother's house.

She arrived to find Dale upright and between beers. His face was puffy as usual, his skin splotched red and brown from six decades of abandoned anger. He nodded gently and tugged his baseball cap as Maisy pulled up, then went back to working on the lawn.

"Are they all dead?" She called out as she slammed her car door. Maisy edged towards Dale, but she made sure to stay close to the house. She didn't want to look for herself. "Where's the queen?"

Dale shrugged, killed the weed whacker, and staked it into the ground like a ski pole. He didn't know anything about bees. Dale hadn't been around yet when they brought the hive home years before, and it was one of the few things he didn't look after here. He said he didn't like to mess with a body that didn't mess with him. In return, the bees left him alone when he dozed near their favorite spot on the porch. Dale's drunken fogs were protracted, but largely harmless. The bees seemed to respect, even admire, the depth of his hazes.

She asked after her mother, and Dale shrugged again, this time more with more resolve. "She's still in that damn jar, Maisy," he muttered, "Right where you left her." He spat into the grass and sighed heavily through his nose.

A brief coldness passed through her gut. "All right, Dale," she breathed. "Let me go see what I can figure out."

Dale looked out towards the road and rubbed the dirt from his hands onto his T-shirt. His fingers were thick and calloused. "What the hell," he rattled as Maisy eased past him.

"I'm not gonna scatter her in the bushes. You want her, take it home with you."

She squinted hard, reminded herself to be patient, and trudged up to the house. For all ten years they were together, Dale had made breakfast for Maisy's mother every morning. When the cancer took her appetite, he brought her green tea instead and waited patiently as she agonized over each sip, all the while aching to get downstairs and have his own first drink of the day. Through all that, and even now after her mother's passing, Dale still kept the lawn mowed, still fixed the pipes when they dripped. He knew it wasn't his house, so Maisy let him stay on for now. It was easier than keeping up two houses by herself. She figured he'd move on soon, maybe go live with his ex-wife in Sevierville. In the meantime, she tried to remind herself that she would be lucky to find a man so devoted, drink or no drink, someday when her own children left her. She paused on the porch to move Dale's cooler off the top step, then went inside to find the apiary handbook.

When the cancer took her appetite, he brought her green tea instead and waited patiently as she agonized over each sip...

Maisy didn't know anything about bees, either, not really. What little she remembered she had learned only by watching her mother, who rarely talked of how or why with any of her garden work. Even those few scraps of knowing were long distant acquisitions, all earned over a decade ago. When her kids were still little, Maisy had moved back home for a year. She finished her GED, then her accounting certificate, riding out the ravages of her divorce and pushing back against whoever tried to stop her. She moved out again as soon as she could afford to, but her mother still liked to tell people that Maisy grew up in this house—twice. She gritted her teeth whenever her mother said things like that. All her mother's friends thought Maisy had a square jaw.

The bees had arrived during that year Maisy and the kids had lived with her mother. Ever since then, the bees had been part of the landscape, a constant whenever she visited. Maisy knew just enough now to suspect the hive was dying. There was nothing to be done, but she hunted in the kitchen cabinets for the book just the same.

■ ■ ■

"I want to get some bees," her mother had said to her. She cuddled Baby Girl in her arms; they were making faces and giggling at each other.

"Momma," Maisy replied, waving at the paper wasps idling under the side porch, "You've got bees."

"You know what I'm talking about," she shot from the side of her mouth. Hunter ran past them, aiming his water pistol at his old tricycle. Her mother touched Hunter's skinny shoulder as he doubled back to growl a militaristic oath at one of his other toys.

"I didn't do it when you were little," she said as Hunter disappeared behind the house. "You were always getting into a mess. Didn't want to listen." Maisy tightened her lips as her mother bounced Baby Girl a time or two. "But these two… My grandchildren need to make some honey."

And so they drove out to Murphy. She knew an organic farmer whose uncle raised bees way out there, just shy of the state line. "Good bees," her mother said, "No chemicals. He's got them so they don't give a damn about anything but making comb."

How the woman knew this, Maisy never thought to ask. They borrowed June's new truck and drove down 74, following the map her mother had drawn on the back of last month's propane bill. June lived next door; she and Maisy's mother had known each other decades, husbands, bodies ago. They talked together like old thieves almost every day and even wore their hair in the same long, grey braids.

Maisy didn't remember how long they all stayed there, or what prices or logistics were negotiated for buying and transporting the hive. That memory was a dozen years old. Perhaps she was told to sit on the porch with her children while all that was accomplished, but she preferred to think she chose to do so.

"You keep the queen, Maisy. But for heaven's sake, be careful with it," her mother chided. She handed over a little cardboard jewelry box and marched back to the truck. Maisy's mother's arms stretched out like wires, unless she was in motion. Then they hung from her like afterthoughts while she plowed on to wherever she was headed. That's how Maisy remembered it—a long arm depositing the queen with her from a distance, then whizzing past. Maisy fumbled with the box, stuffed it deep in the pocket of her favorite hoodie, and trudged along behind.

The transaction itself had not been memorable enough for Maisy to keep with her, but she did recall the ride home. Her mother drove. The hive sat in the bed of the truck, and Hunter and Baby Girl napped on the tiny back seat in the cab. The engine revved all the way back up home while her mother went on and on.

"No chemicals, the man said. I'll just use a little menthol and thyme when I need to." She twinkled her eyes in the rearview mirror at Maisy's kids. "We'll smoke them out when they're good and ready," she chirped, "and have us a little treat for those grandbabies soon."

Maisy looked out the window and watched the mountains darken around her. She could think only of the queen in her hand. Maisy felt small, like she could fit into the back seat with her children. Rarely were such important items entrusted to her. She wanted to look at the queen so badly, to study it while it was alone, away from the colony, but she didn't. Her mother would kill her if it flew away, so Maisy kept her hand inside the fluffy pocket, holding the box close to her. The whole thing felt like it mattered somehow, so for all the things she forgot, she remembered that part.

Her mother dithered and fretted over the hive for a few days, and then it was like they had always been there. Maisy's kids never feared the bees or ran from them. They were just always around, hovering and tending to their own concerns. "They sure have settled right in, haven't they?" her mother beamed one morning as she watched a fat worker stagger out of a peony.

■ ■ ■

A few months later, after it got hot outside, staying that way even into the early morning, her mother called June over from next door, and the two women worked out a plan for harvesting the honey. They had no centrifuge or fancy equipment, so instead they drank scuppernong wine and remembered their childhoods until they settled on the best method they knew. June had a mask and an ancient smoker, so they fetched those and told Maisy to keep the children inside no matter what. Maisy had no idea what they were doing out there; she could only see so much from the house.

Soon the kitchen came alive with giggles and movement. Her mother put a huge sieve and a clean plastic bucket in the sink. She grabbed some kind of putty knife and told Hunter to help her scrape the comb off the frames. Hunter quickly took to being trusted with such a grownup-looking job, and soon the sieve was overflowing as the honey drained slowly into the bucket.

"Now," her mother said to her son and Baby Girl with great portent, "Now, we squish!"

The children took turns squeezing the comb and squealing. Maisy took over when Baby Girl tried to put her head in the bucket. The warm ooze of wax and honey on Maisy's hands felt like some old, fine thing she knew well, even though her mother had never allowed her such pleasures when she was little. She continued to squish, dimly registering June's reminders to save the beeswax for her.

When Maisy turned from the bucket to wipe her hands, she saw her mother handing down a bit of comb to Baby Girl. The toddler stood, wide eyed and enraptured, one hand almost entirely in her mouth while the other hand reached up,

The warm ooze of wax and honey on Maisy's hands felt like some old, fine thing she knew well, even though her mother had never allowed her such pleasures when she was little.

the rest of her as still as earth, for that scrap of sweet. Every inch of Baby Girl was covered in honey. In her hair, down her back, between her toes—it was as if she had rolled in the stuff. June laughed and hooted as she leaned against the door frame, egging everyone on. Maisy could only think of getting both children into the bathtub as quickly as possible.

All told, the sticky chaos of their first harvest yielded barely a gallon. The following year, her mother and June refined their technique. The honey came just after Maisy moved with the kids into a new duplex in Waynesville. Maisy liked her job, and the children could go to a good school, one with computer labs and a real football team. Her mother dropped off four big jars as a housewarming gift, and for months the kids insisted on putting "goo"—butter and honey stirred together—on their toast every morning.

Dale showed up a little while later. He built a new shed, made her mother laugh, and settled into the deck chair on the porch. The bees continued as ever. For the next few summers, Hunter would ask to go over the mountain and help his grandmother with the hive. Maisy usually just dropped him off. His first year at Haywood Middle, Hunter went to Vacation Bible School camp and missed the honey harvest. After that the bees rarely caught his attention. When he made the high school varsity football team and had to practice through the summers, he stopped visiting his grandmother's house altogether. All he wanted was a football scholarship, a ticket out of town.

■ ■ ■

Last year, right after her mother's diagnosis, Hunter packed off to college in Georgia, and two of June's four hives died. The frames came up empty, light as anything when she lifted them out. Maisy's mother comforted her old friend and offered her a jar from her own stores. She did not mention her own illness. Maisy brought them both a glass of iced tea and sat down nearby to sort through a pile of doctor bills while they talked. June kept worrying aloud, her voice high pitched and endless.

"Oh, what is it, I wonder?" June keened. "What's making them leave the queen like that? Do they just... do they get lost?" She kept staring out the kitchen windows, red eyed, bobbing her greying head as if hoping to see a swarm of familiar faces. June wrapped her arms around herself inside a ragged blue button-down shirt that had belonged to some husband or another. Then she started quoting Shakespeare; something about sitting on the ground and telling sad stories about dead kings. Maisy had to chew her pencil to keep from getting up and swatting her.

"There, now," her mother had said. "I'm sure none of it's your doing, honey."

■ ■ ■

This year, in all the bother and confusion of watching her mother die, Maisy had forgotten to ask how June's remaining hives were faring. It was spring, and she had had bigger things on her mind. Taxes would soon be overdue on her mother's house, and no one could find the insurance policy for the car. The apiary guide had apparently disappeared, too. Anyway, Dale said June hadn't been stopping by so often like she used to. Neither had Maisy, but Dale didn't say anything about that.

As Maisy rifled through the kitchen cabinets for the beekeeper's book, she glanced into the dining room at the pewter urn sitting on the mantel. Her face reddened. Maisy lowered her hands and looked away, out a window into the side yard. "Momma," she whispered, "You've got to tell me where you *keep* things."

Maisy thought she'd better go up and check on her mother's room. Perhaps the book was there, and she could tidy up a little, water the plants. The upstairs hall was a long series of doors. All the bedrooms were tiny and hot; in the summer, half the doors swelled in the heat and sealed themselves shut.

On the stairs, a weight overtook her. Lately, Maisy had made it her job to check the progress of the seedlings on the bedroom sill during her visits. But she found today that she was ready to let them go. Whether there were tomatoes to plant this year didn't matter. Dale would forget to tend them, or accidentally mow them, and she had little time for canning even if they did survive until their fruit ripened. Maisy shook her head. Only six weeks since her mother's funeral, and already the whole house had been abandoned.

She rested her hand on the banister, smoothed it up and down slowly, and decided to leave things as they were. She needed to get home. Her daughter was supposed to cook a "traditional" family dinner this week and document the process in her journal for English class. So far the preparations had been disastrous, with Baby Girl huffing and brooding in a cloud of corn flour and teenage angst.

She returned to the kitchen and puttered through the cabinets, hoping her son would come home from college for spring break. She paused in the breakfast nook and looked out the big window to watch Dale unlocking the shed. Maisy figured he kept working on the yard for the same reason she still changed the sheets on Hunter's bed every week. It was something to do, a muscle memory. Just like whenever Maisy drove to Asheville and got scared in all that traffic. With every near miss and honked horn, she'd reach her hand out to the empty seat beside her, just in case, to protect phantom children long gone from the passenger seat.

In between the panes as she looked out, Maisy spotted a shriveled drone pawing meekly at the glass. Her eyes focused on the sills and screens all along the big window. Scores of drunken, half dead insects lay writhing alongside the curled husks of their comrades who had already succumbed. Maisy stared for a long while and wondered where the thousands of others had gone, whether they were sick, or dead, or just forgot where home was. She blinked and thought about the sound they used to make when all was in bloom.

Tomorrow, or maybe the next day, if she remembered to, she would ask June about her hives. *If the rest of June's bees are dying, too,* Maisy thought, *if they've got the same sickness, well, I guess I'll take it as some kind of a sign.*

Outside, Dale fired up the lawnmower. The house filled with a low, angry buzz. Maisy glided through the house and out onto the porch, closed her eyes, and waited for the smell of fresh-cut grass to come to her. She hovered in that moment alone and familiar, and almost forgot her plans to leave.

Her phone vibrated angrily in her pocket. She reached for it, read her daughter's text, and thumped down the front steps to her car. Barely looking at the keypad, or Dale, at or the house behind her, Maisy let her fingers click and dance their reply: *Yes, Baby Girl. Forget cooking. I'll take us into town for supper.* ■

76

TELEPHONE

I.
An appendage of my stepdaughter's hand,
pink as the tongue it has muted.
Even as she sleeps
it snores gently in her loosened grasp.
All day her thumbs tap
coded words across the screen,
her eyes alive in its light.

II.
In my mother's hand,
another riddle she once knew
how to solve. Today she is
all thumbs as numbers
shine like ciphers
others must unlock.

III.
In my dreams it sits calm
and ample as the Sphinx
upon a table and I
fumble frantic at the dial
that will not make
its circle. Hello,
hello, I call into its
dull hum.

PAULETTA HANSEL

FAMILIAL TREMORS

My mother's hands
pinned patterns she unfolded,
thin brown
as last year's leaves,
onto cotton, rayon, double-knit, velvet,
wool for our coats
laid out on the maple table
with extra leaves
bought with the dollars and coins
her sewing had earned.
Her hands pinned hems and seams
as we stood (Straight, now!)
on chairs wearing
the cloth cut neat,
wrote checks for what
they could not make and
kept the family books that tracked
that money in and out again.
Those hands could not
keep still even when she sat,
made lace
for the table
with thick needles and thread.
On slow days
they'd polish the silver
we seldom used.

Today my mother
holds out her hands
to show me how they

tremble, leaves
about to fall, they'll not
steady now for pin or pen.
She pulls
them close again
as hands would soothe
some dream-shivered child—
    Rest now.
    Day's done.

PAULETTA HANSEL

MOUNTAIN FATALISM IN WILEY CASH'S *A Land More Kind Than Home*

ERICA ABRAMS LOCKLEAR

In 2003 Wiley Cash had the initial idea for the storyline of his debut novel, *A Land More Kind Than Home,* when his "professor, Reggie Scott Young, brought in a news story about a young African American boy with autism who'd been smothered during a healing service on Chicago's South Side." Cash elaborates that he "wanted to tell the story, but [he'd] never been to Chicago and knew [he] couldn't represent the experience of those living on the South Side.[1]

Instead, Cash set the novel in Madison County, a region in Western North Carolina that has long been associated with both positive and negative stereotypes about Appalachia.

On the positive side, those interested in traditional ballads often connect the county with the hit movie *Songcatcher*, since both Olive Dame Campbell and Cecil Sharp collected ballads in the area in the nineteen-teens. Photographers Rob Amberg and Tim Barnwell have also documented the beauty of the landscape and its people in their image collections, while musicians including Laura Boosinger and Sheila Kay Adams have brought major recognition to the area for its performance arts. Adams, for example, was recently named a 2013 National Endowment for the Arts National Heritage Fellow, one of only nine in the United States.

But Madison County also seems to function as a distinctly Appalachian space onto which cultural anxieties about poverty, drug use, unruly evangelicalism, and all manner of negative stereotypes are projected. It was the site of the Shelton Laurel Massacre in 1863, garnering the nickname "Bloody Madison" that still resonates today. In 2009, for example, journalist Rob Neufeld wrote an article for the *Asheville Citizen-Times* newspaper about a true-crime novel called *Unfinished Business* by Mark Pinsky. The novel re-creates the unsolved rape and murder of a VISTA worker, Nancy Morgan, in Madison County in 1970. According to Neufeld, a Madison County native named Ellen Banks told Pinsky, "We'll never really rest in Madison County about Nancy's death. People really liked her," and "We've had enough problems since the Shelton Laurel massacre."[2] Banks' mention

1 Hovis, George, "'The Seen and the Unseen': An Interview with Wiley Cash," *North Carolina Literary Review* 22 (2013), 94.

2 Neufeld, Rob, "True Crime Book Digs into Unsolved 1970 Madison Rape-Murder," *Asheville Citizen-Times,* May 27, 2009.

of the massacre—almost one-hundred-and-fifty years after the incident—signals that residents remain acutely aware of the associations people inside and outside of the region make between the county and violence. I often tell my students that Madison County serves the same purpose for North Carolina that West Virginia serves for the rest of the nation. Scholars including Anthony Harkins and J.W. Williamson have hypothesized that the rest of the nation—or in this case, the rest of the state—uses such areas to imagine a population of "them, not us," prompting Manly Wade Wellman to write in 1973 that Madison County was "surely among the most misunderstood and most interesting of all counties in North Carolina," and certainly that still holds true today.[3]

This classic blend of binaries perpetuated since the late 1800s of the rustic pioneer inhabiting the same beautiful mountainous space as the degenerate hillbilly coupled with a rich history of Civil War conflict, tourism, and a little-known World War I internment camp serves as rich literary fodder for contemporary authors: Charles Frazier, for example, sets several scenes of *Thirteen Moons* at the Warm Springs Hotel, while writers including but not limited to Pamela Duncan, Terry Roberts, Rose McLarney, and Ron Rash place much of their fiction and poetry in the county. The fact that Wiley Cash uses Madison County as the setting for his novel about a snake-handling congregation who smothers a boy to death while trying to heal him of his muteness (though readers soon learn that the preacher's motivations are likely far more sinister) is a loaded one. At first glance, it might seem as though the novel perpetuates problematic notions about the county: after all, where else would one find a stereotypical Western North Carolina snake-handling congregation in the 1980s? But a closer inspection reveals that much more is at play in Cash's novel than a too-easy reliance on clichés of mountain people and their religious practices. Instead, Cash first draws readers in by perhaps giving them what they might expect to find in a novel set in Madison County, but he soon turns those expectations on their head.

This tactic has no doubt been successful; the novel has received stunningly positive reviews, quickly garnering a spot on the *New York Times* bestseller list and a recent appearance on the shortlist for the Robert W. Bingham PEN Literary Award. Combining elements of Southern Gothic, literary thriller, and familiar Appalachian tropes, the novel finds easy refuge in already established traditions that casual readers and literary critics alike find attractive. In some cases this widespread appeal means that reviewers are perhaps too eager to group the text with its Southern, not Appalachian, predecessors. *Kirkus Reviews*, for example, states that the novel "explores Faulkner/O'Connor country, a place where folks endure a hard life by clinging to God's truths echoing from hardscrabble churches."[4] While certain literary elements of Cash's novel clearly harken back to techniques employed by both William Faulkner and Flannery O'Connor, the geographic location Cash chooses of Western North Carolina hardly equates to Faulkner's Mississippi or O'Connor's southern Georgia. Even so, the larger point that the novel fits within the canon of Southern literature is a valid one.

What critical attention the book has received thus far focuses on the influence literary giants like Thomas Wolfe had on Cash's writing. George Hovis, for example, places *A Land More Kind*

3 Wellman, Manly Wade, *The Kingdom of Madison: A Southern Mountain Fastness and Its People* (Chapel Hill: University of North Carolina Press, 1973), 3.

4 "A Land More Kind Than Home," a review of *A Land More Kind Than Home* by Wiley Cash, *Kirkus Review*, April 3, 2012, https://www.kirkusreviews.com/book-reviews/wiley-cash/land-more-kind-than-home

than Home, Terry Roberts's *A Short Time to Stay Here*, and Ron Rash's *The Cove* firmly within the tradition of Appalachian literature while noting the ways in which each diverge from Wolfe's frequent urban settings.[5] Certainly Cash's novel qualifies as Appalachian in other ways too, but it also forges new and important literary ground by upending one long-held stereotype of Appalachia in particular: mountain fatalism.

Religion scholars and philosophers have written extensively about the term "fatalism." Regardless of whether it is defined in religious or secular terms, at its most basic level, fatalism means that an outcome is predetermined. Southern religion scholar Deborah Vansau McCauley explains that "the extreme Calvinist position of extreme predestination" is "the closest doctrinal formulation to what can be characterized as 'fatalism.'"[6] According to philosopher Robert Solomon, "fatalism is the narrative thesis that some action or event was bound to happen because it 'fits' so well with the agent's character," suggesting that the outcome may be positive or negative.[7] It is simply what was meant to be. But when we add the qualifier "mountain" to the term, the definition takes on a decidedly negative connotation.

This regional understanding of the term began early, as evidenced in William Goodell Frost's frequently cited *Atlantic Monthly* article from 1899, "Our Contemporary Ancestors." In it, he writes that the "the mountains seem the natural home of fatalism," suggesting a kind of predetermined quality to a specific geographic location.[8] Almost a century later, War on Poverty writer Jack Weller compounded statements like Frost's by contending that "[t]he fatalism of mountain people has a religious quality to it: 'If that's the way God wants it, I reckon that's the way it'll be. We just have to take what the Lord sends us. He knows best.'"[9] The term is used still used widely; for example, in a 2011 article about how fatalism affects healthcare in Appalachia, Wendy Welch writes that it can appear as "Faith-based; oppositional to distrust; pride covering poverty; apathy or unwillingness to change; based on ignorance of potential health outcomes; upholding a quality of life." She concludes with a plea for "an ongoing dialogue about care in Appalachia" that will help dismantle "the smothering blanket of fatalistic stereotypes."[10] Although Cash's novel does not focus on healthcare in the region, it nevertheless helps us begin having the kind of dialogue that Welch recommends.

It does so because in a literary sense, a character in Appalachian fiction with a fatalistic outlook would automatically expect the worst. Or as Janet Boggess Welch explains, "It is Murphy's Law of the Mountains that things will always get worse, even if presently they are better."[11] This propensity for gloom is somewhat understandable given the often difficult living circumstances for some—though notably not all—in the mountains from the late 1800s to present-day, yet the focus on this outlook in literature seems unusually common. In Mary Noailles Murfree's 1883 local color short story, "The Harnt That Walks Chilhowhee," for example, Clarsie

5 Hovis, George, "The Legacy of Thomas Wolfe in Contemporary Appalachian Fiction: Four Recent North Carolina Novels," *Thomas Wolfe Review* 36.1/2 (2012): 70-91

6 McCauley, Deborah Vansau, *Appalachian Mountain Religion: A History* (Champaign-Urbana: University of Illinois Press, 1995), 97.

7 Solomon, Robert C, "On Fate and Fatalism," *Philosophy East and West* 53.4 (2003): 447.

8 Frost, William Goodell, "Our Contemporary Ancestors in the Southern Mountains," *The Atlantic Monthly* 83.497 (1899): 317.

9 Weller, Jack E., *Yesterday's People: Life in Contemporary Appalachia* (Lexington: The University Press of Kentucky, 1965), 37-38.

10 Welch, Wendy, "Self Control, Fatalism, and Health in Appalachia," *Journal of Appalachian Studies* 17.1/2 (2011): 109, 119-120.

11 Welch, Janet Boggess, "Uneven Ground: Cultural Values, Moral Standards, and Religiosity in the Heart of Appalachia," *Christianity in Appalachia: Profiles in Regional Pluralism,* ed. Bill J. Leonard (Knoxville: University of Tennessee Press, 1999), 56.

Giles' mother laments that "Some folks is the favored of the Lord, an' t' others hev ter work fur everything an' git nuthin'. Waal, waal; we-uns will see our reward in the nex' worl'."[12] Here Clarsie's mother does appear to have some hope for the future, but this better end may only be realized after her death and even then, nothing is guaranteed. Her perspective is one grounded in religion, but in a much more secular, contemporary example, former-teacher-turned-drug-dealer Leonard Schuler in Ron Rash's Madison County-based novel, *The World Made Straight,* questions whether landscape is destiny. In other words, his character asks tough questions about the potential to improve his lot in life when living in Madison County, where he feels surrounded on all sides by mountains that limit his view of the world, both literally and figuratively. Likewise, in a recent essay in *Southern Cultures,* poet Michael McFee writes: "Sometimes, after I make an especially dark pronouncement or gloomy prediction, I'll shrug and say, 'Well, I'm just a hillbilly fatalist.' I inherited that philosophical predisposition from my mother, who could find the coal-black lining in any silver cloud. She believed, and a lifetime of disappointing experience have proved, that fate was waiting for you at every turn, ready to crush your spirits and prospects flatter than a fritter: you might as well accept it and submit to it."[13] From turn-of-the-century writing about Appalachia to War on Poverty reports about the region to contemporary literature, the phrase "mountain fatalism" signals an unavoidably undesirable conclusion.

These examples represent only a fraction of the many references to mountain fatalism in Appalachian literature, thus readers familiar with other mountain writers might expect Cash's characters to share this fatalistic outlook, but not all of them do. In fact, one major way in which Cash subverts reader expectations is by joining with other writers who break with Appalachian literary tradition when he depicts surprisingly hopeful characters, despite the exceedingly difficult situations in which they find themselves. In doing so he overturns proclamations like Weller's that "Mountaineers are never very optimistic about anything."[14] Ironically, although religion seems intimately connected to a fatalistic outlook in much, though not all, previous fictional and non-fictional writing about Appalachia, for Cash the kind of faith he writes about has the opposite result. He states in an interview that "What's amazing about the charismatic faith or the holiness movement is that everyone is considered morally corrupt. And you can be morally corrupt and pray your way out of it. You can be the greatest sinner in the world and then ask for forgiveness. You credit your successes to God and your failures to the Devil."[15] While this doctrinal belief is certainly not new to Appalachia, Cash's representation of it as a central feature in his novel lends hope to what seems an otherwise hopeless situation comprised of a majority of characters seeking spiritual and human assurance. In this way, the novel features an ending that combines both tragedy and cautious optimism.

The story opens from Adelaide Lyle's perspective, an elderly woman who feels partially responsible for the death of Stump Hall during a church service. Early in her section we learn about the change that her church underwent ten years prior when a former meth-maker, Carson Chambliss, became pastor. She explains that he changed the church's name from French Broad Church of Christ to River Road Church of Christ in Signs and painted Mark 16:17-18 as a scripture reference on the church sign. Although Cash does not include the scripture

12 Murfree, Mary Noailles, "The 'Harnt' That Walks Chilhowee," *In the Tennessee Mountains* (Knoxville: University of Tennessee Press, 1970), 293.

13 McFee, Michael, "My Inner Hillbilly," *Southern Cultures* 19.2 (2013): 63.

14 Weller, 38.

15 Rocca, Alexander, "His Brother's Keeper," *Publishers Weekly* 259.10 (2012): 46.

in the chapter, readers familiar with the Bible know that it reads as such: "And these signs shall follow them that believe; In my name shall they cast out devils; they shall speak with new tongues; they shall take up serpents; and if they drink any deadly thing, it shall not hurt them; they shall lay hands on the sick, and they shall recover." Lyle goes on to recount an incident when Chambliss first introduced snake handling to the congregation and a woman named Molly Jameson died. After that incident, Lyle took care of the children during services, explaining "I had my little congregation and he had his, and we didn't have hardly anything to do with each other. I felt like I was doing what the Lord wanted me to do with those children."[16] Given her devotion to these children, Lyle feels especially guilty when Christopher Hall, whom everyone else in the novel except his mother calls Stump, dies.

Likewise, the novel's other two narrators—Stump's brother, Jess, and the town's Sherriff, Clem Barefield—are also seeking a kind of redemption, but for different reasons. While Lyle feels guilty about her inability to save Stump, Jess feels ashamed because he witnesses two significant incidents that contribute his brother's death: first, Stump and Jess accidentally discover that their mother, Julie, is having an affair with Carson Chambliss. Jess flees the scene without detection by Chambliss, but Stump does not. Cash's portrayal of Chambliss as an ex-drug-dealing, immoral preacher makes clear that both Jess and readers should be concerned for Stump's well-being, yet Jess is reluctant to tell anyone what he and Stump saw. Second, when Jess and his friend Joe Bill sneak to the back of the church and peep through a gap above the air conditioner, they witness the first of two healing ceremonies performed on Stump. Traumatized by seeing Stump "kicking like he was trying to get away," Jess "for a second for[gets] where [he is] and holler[s] out 'Mama!'"[17] Jess' mother hears the call and interprets it as a miracle, believing that the laying of hands has made Stump able to speak. Jess does not reveal the truth to his mother, and when Stump dies during the second healing service that evening, Jess is left harboring not one, but two dark secrets.

The novel's third narrator, Clem Barefield, also carries an enormous sense of guilt, one that ties him to Jess' grandfather, Jimmy Hall. A notorious drunk with a history of physical and verbal abuse, Jimmy Hall once supervised Clem's son, Jeff, who dies in a tragic power line accident. Clem blames himself for letting Jeff work with Jimmy, and after a long hiatus from Madison County, Jimmy returns in an effort to rebuild his relationship with his family. Cash manages to connect this cast of characters through a shared sense of responsibility, guilt, and a yearning for forgiveness. Despite these desperate longings, the novel ends in tragedy: Jess tells his father about his mother's affair, resulting in a shoot-out near the novel's conclusion that leaves both Jess' father and Carson Chambliss dead and Jess' mother injured and traumatized. Jess' prospects for the future look grim with a mother who seems likely to abandon him and a grandfather-turned-caretaker with a history of addiction and abuse.

Moreover, given the fatalistic tradition into which this novel falls, readers might expect the remaining characters to feel dejected and hopeless. Instead, in an unexpected twist that plunges into surprising territory for Appalachian characters, Cash suggests that perhaps both Jimmy Hall and Adelaide Lyle find something that resembles forgiveness or at least the possibility of it. Jimmy Hall's return to Madison County coincides with Stump's death, so his attempt to re-enter the family structure occurs as the family grieves and tries

16 Cash, Wiley, *A Land More Kind Than Home* (New York: William Morrow, 2012), 13.

17 Ibid., 50.

to understand how and why Stump died. Cash makes clear that Julie does not approve of Jimmy's return when she tells her husband, Ben, "Well, if he asks you for any money, then you'd better tell him to get in line behind me."[18] Jess meets his grandfather for the first time when the sheriff and Jess' father realize that they need someone to take care of Jess as they attempt to sort out what happened to Stump. On the ride to Jess' house, Jess notices that Jimmy's fingers are twitching, and when Jimmy tries to buy alcohol at a gas station (but fails because it is Sunday), then searches the house for hidden bottles, readers understand the severity of his dependence on alcohol.

From this point forward readers might expect a swift decline into addiction for Jimmy, but instead, Cash includes a reference that signals hope for Jimmy when he successfully removes a splinter from Jess' hand. During the process Jimmy explains that he has experience working with wood, and when Jess asks him if he is a carpenter—which when read within the context of this novel may be seen as a reference to Jesus—Jimmy responds, "I ain't much of anything right now ... but I've been a lot of things. I guess I was one of those at one time."[19] Though Jimmy feels insecure about his standing, Cash nevertheless embeds a powerful reference to forgiveness and the hope for eternal life with this comparison to Jesus' occupation. Such referencing makes sense when paired with Carson Chambliss' Satan-like portrayal; after one particularly unsettling encounter with him, Adelaide reveals that she had "looked right into the face of evil."[20] This comparison seems even more appropriate given Chambliss' dependence upon snakes in his church services; in the same way that a serpent disrupts the Garden of Eden, so too does Chambliss disrupt life in the novel's community.

Yet Cash's characters are not doomed to suffer the evils of the world, nor of Carson Chambliss. Although the novel ends in tragedy, Jess seems to undergo a kind of baptism, or at least cleansing, when he is caught in a rain storm on the way home from Joe Bill's and decides to tell his father the truth about his mother's affair. Moreover, in the novel's conclusion Adelaide observes that at Ben Hall's funeral, Jimmy "had him on a nice clean shirt and a tie just like his grandson's" and he "kept those hands steady," a sign that he had not been drinking that day." Lyle goes on to report, "Jimmy Hall brings [Jess] down for church just about every Sunday now, but he never comes with him," yet she decides "that's all right with [her]. He don't ever have to step foot inside [the] church if he doesn't want to. It's enough for [her] to know that he's out there if Jess needs him. [She] think[s] it's enough for Jess too." Her comments about Jimmy are notably free of judgment, and Adelaide also states, "A church can be healed, and it can be saved like people can be saved. And that's what happened to us."[21] Certainly the perspective with which Cash ends the novel does not coincide with "Murphy's Law of the Mountains." Instead, Adelaide's narration provides a rupture of optimism within what seems an otherwise bleak situation. This tentative hopefulness echoes the ending of James Still's seminal Appalachian novel *River of Earth*, when the Baldridge family rejoices in the birth of a new child, even though their last child likely starved to death or Charles Frazier's *Cold Mountain*, where grieving Ada finds joy in a new baby. Like Still and Frazier, Cash avoids giving readers a sugar-coated ending but instead imbues a dire situation with the possibility—however unlikely—of a better day for his characters. ■

18 Ibid., 75.
19 Ibid., 145.
20 Ibid., 228.
21 Ibid., 304, 306, 305.

ROAD'S END

Whom have I in heaven but thee? and there is nothing else upon earth that I desire beside thee. —Psalm 73:25, RSV

The road, crowned with undisturbed gravel,
where once a killdeer dared build
a nest, lay four grey mottled eggs,
each pivoted toward an unmarked center,
the road runs off between fescue.
It comes first through deciduous forest,
where maple and sweet gum leaves wet
the road into miry slickness,
clatters over a wood-slatted bridge,
before it emerges in daylight,
curves toward the house. Windows
wink. Thoughts of chenille bedspreads,
a gliding rocker on the screened porch,
clear well water, a saucepan rocking
on the stove's hot eye, yellow custard
from the cream of a Guernsey's milk,
all wink from memory.

Such undisclosed gravel lanes,
grey road dust hazing into distances,
where white houses pose in old yards
of forsythia, lilac, jonquils,
draw me to country pastorates.
Each pathway is a one-way passage,
emotions preserved like can goods.
But I've seen too many sterilized kitchens, home health
care beds,
tight-faced, nervous women.

Some still work a garden, but laughter
went over the treetops with the baseballs
of wild teenage sons. A silence has fallen,
a dry rusty uncurling of a road, mailbox
at one end and gaunt house at the other.
I marvel at the strength of faith here,
at the lonesome stillness of longsuffering.

CHARLES A. SWANSON

BOOK REVIEWS

Marie Manilla. *The Patron Saint of Ugly.* **Boston, Mass.: Mariner Books, 2014. 352 pages. Softcover. $13.95.**

Reviewed by Grace Toney Edwards

At first glance, the brilliant red popping out of a blue sky on the cover of Marie Manilla's novel *The Patron Saint of Ugly* flows like a cloak, but is actually a mane of red hair with only one aquamarine eye peeking out of a face. *Why are tiny figures of elderly women and young children climbing the mass of hair, as though it were a crimson hillside?* one might ask on further study. But once the reader moves into the book itself, she soon learns that the cover supplies a dominant image for the novel.

Protagonist Garnet Ferrari, colloquially known as Saint Garnet, tells the story through a series of twenty-one audio tapes she is recording for an investigation being conducted by the Vatican to determine whether she really does have healing powers, as the masses assert. A young twenty-something, she disavows all such claims. In her first tape addressed "To the Congregation for the Causes of Saints, Archbishop Gormley in particular," she says, "Before we begin, Archie, I want to reiterate that the only reason I've granted this intrusion is that the sooner we dispel this sainted nonsense the sooner I can reclaim my life, or perhaps claim it for the first time."

Garnet goes on to recount various healing miracles that have been attributed to her from the time she was four-years-old. She continually maintains, however, that she is not doing "it"—if anyone is, it's Nonna, her Sicilian grandmother, who just as vociferously maintains it is not she. With this conflict, Manilla establishes one of the many dualities that operate throughout the book: both Garnet and Nonna seem to be present when "miracles" occur, the former unwillingly and the latter quite willingly. Garnet is young and sassy; Nonna is old and feisty in her own way. Garnet scoffs at the rituals and trappings of Catholicism; Nonna embraces them (both the Old Religion of pagan superstitions and the New Religion of current practices). Where Nonna was considered to be a beautiful young woman, red-haired like the Pining Nereid of the Strait of Messina, Garnet is considered to be ugly because of the multiple wine-colored birthmarks that cover her entire body, along with her flaming red hair. The birthmarks, which look strangely like identifiable land masses from across the world, have given rise to the "Santa Garney" reputation, based on the Sicilian legend of Saint Garnet del Vulcano who survived an eruption of Mount Etna, only to be left with red splotches all over her body and the ability to heal skin disorders. Nonna told this legend to Garnet at a young age, indicating her great love for this special child. She went on to spread it throughout the neighborhood, citing the connections, of course, to her own granddaughter. Perhaps it was Nonna's attempt to make the marked child more accepted by the townspeople; whatever her motive, Garnet lives from the outset as "the other."

While this book sparkles with humor and wit in the monologue of Garnet and the dialogue of the various characters, it also tells of hard times caused by physical imperfections, by abusive relatives, by cruel townspeople,

Garnet goes on to recount various healing miracles that have been attributed to her from the time she was four-years-old. She continually maintains, however, that she is not doing "it"...

and by withered dreams. Many of these struggles play out through the dualities that Manilla so skillfully employs: the village is populated half by Italians and half by Irish, both groups devout Catholics worshipping at the same church but each set needing its own saints and rituals. Garnet's parents demonstrate a similar dichotomy: her father Angelo is a short dark Italian; her mother Marina a tall blonde of British ancestry. Angelo comes from working-class immigrants from Calabria and Sicily who have settled in Sweetwater, West Virginia; Marina comes from wealth and privilege, a huge estate in Charlottesville, Virginia, and a year at Smith College. Angelo's parents represent yet another duality. Back in Italy two brothers fell in love with the same girl, the beautiful red-haired Diamante (Nonna). She loved the younger brother Angelo who wanted to marry her and grow sweet-grape vineyards on the Sicilian hillsides, but through deceit and trickery, Dominick forced Diamante to marry him and immediately spirited her off to America to a life of domination and toil. They produced two sons, also named Dominick and Angelo. Like their namesakes, they were destined to play out the roles of dominating older brother and subservient never-quite-good-enough younger brother. From an early age Garnet suffers from the emotional trauma her father endures, both because she senses his pain and because she longs for the love that he cannot seem to give.

Although family members are the major characters—both saints and villains—in the story, one outsider plays a small but significant role. She is La Strega, the rich widow who lives at the top of Dagowop Hill in a huge house behind gates and fences. She never mixes with the commoners, but she keeps a close eye on them via her powerful telescope and the research of her beleaguered servant Radisson. Through strange and unbelievable, yet comical, twists of fate, her estate eventually becomes Garnet's home, the location from which she first entertains Archbishop Gormley and then records the twenty-one tapes that detail her life.

Manilla excels in *The Patron Saint of Ugly* with a plot filled with family conflicts that readers can easily relate to and with a liberal sprinkling of Italian-spiced dialect and cultural traits adding both humor and realism. She layers riches into the mix with her utilization of contrasts and recurring images such as electrical current, water, and statuary that connect to Garnet and Nonna's mysterious "gifts." The somewhat artificial device of telling the story through audio tapes could become stiff or forced, but one never feels that—like any good epistolary novelist, Manilla manages to make the device almost disappear, yet maintains it as a sturdy frame encasing the whole, allowing her talents as a storyteller to shine. ■

Charles Dodd White. *A Shelter of Others.* **Peninsula, Ohio: Fiddleback ltd, 2014. 216 pages. Softcover. $14.00.**

Reviewed by Jane Hicks

Whether we are born into a family or make a family, the urge to reside in a tribe is strong. So says Charles Dodd White in his novel *A Shelter of Others*. From the elderly Sam Laws, who lived a wonderful life as a child, to Mason, his son, who was neglected for Sam's academic career, each character in this book seeks a familial bond with someone. As the groups coalesce, the tension builds.

After his release from prison for running pills, Mason Laws returns home with only a vague notion of how to start a new life. His wife, Lavada, never came to see him the two years he was in prison, but continued to take excellent care of Sam, Mason's father. Sam is in the late stages of dementia and his care has occupied her time and resources for the period of time Mason has been away. He calls her daughter and usually accepts her wishes. If he doesn't properly medicate, Sam becomes like a willful and unpredictable child.

Mason does not immediately go to town, but sets up shelter in a ruined lumber camp on the mountain above his old home. He eventually finds work and a place to live with Hammond, the owner of a rundown grocery store and a building of dilapidated apartments. Mason helps run the store and refurbish the apartments and Hammond gives him a place to live. He also takes of care of Irving, a crippled man found squatting on Hammond's property. They form a makeshift family, much as Sam and Lavada have.

White lets the story unfold and then wrap about itself again as the characters run a collision course. His beautiful language is most evident when Sam speaks to the reader in his lucid voice with chapters interspersed through the book. He has been a neglectful father, favoring his career as an English professor and Hawthorne scholar over his son. Sam also dwells on his own childhood. "My curse, I realize now as an old man, has been that I should have known such happiness so early in this wrecking life." His last chapter, however, shows his worst imaginings and launches a literal and figurative storm that brings them all to calamity.

White's main characters occupy the pages with authority. We realize Mason, Lavada, and Sam's motivation and madness. Three other pivotal characters seem less developed and the reader wants more. Dennis, Lavada's boss and possible love interest, Cody Gibbs, the deputy, and Irving, the old man Mason and Hammond bring into their circle, feel less realized. White's sparse and beautiful telling has room for more. The spare nature of the book (a little over two hundred pages) contains a compelling story and moves it to the conclusion. However, this also leaves the reader wanting, especially in the case of Deputy Gibbs.

The novel shows a gritty, anti-pastoral side of Appalachia but one not without hope. The characters find sanctuary in the families they create for themselves—the shelter of others—and in community. As Deputy Gibbs' father says, "I know it's hard to find people in this world," he said. "It's so hard to tell them what it means when you see something familiar in the other." So the survivors continue, as they make their way and find the familiar in others.

A Shelter of Others explores the concept of family and home in the setting of a rural and isolated Appalachia. From the cabin on the edge of the national forest, to a small river town, the characters struggle with rugged landscape, both internal and external. This is not a pastoral setting but one of wild beauty and danger. It is in that rugged setting that the characters' needs collide, the survivors already looking toward finding home. ■

THE FOX THAT LIVES BY THE ZOO

He trots past the lion's enclosure
He knows in his foxy brain
the big tawny fellow can't reach him,
Sometimes the cat paces on the edge of the pit
beyond the wire, sometimes casts his yellow stare,
sometimes shows a wet, white fang.
The fox takes all this in.

He visits the zoo to fill his nostrils
with the scent of bloody beef tossed to
the cats by men behind that little door.

In the dark, he slithers under the wire,
clips down the pavement where humans walk.
His nose leads to scraps of burgers and greasy fries.
He does not linger. He scents the stench
of creatures too long confined.

On his side of the wire, he loathes the house cats
who invade his woods, hunters as twitchy
as the sparrows they long to snag. He does
not kill these cats, but leaps over them, nipping,
running them to their porches, where they primp
and loll, affecting feline indifference.

His side of the wire, life is a long stalk
Often, the mouse skitters away, the bird
taunts from high branches, the clenched stomach sours.
Out here he must gamble with prowling coyotes,

snapping traps, aimless boys with stupid rifles.
Once, he saw the lion mount a female, seize her
by the nape, his massive haunches rolling,
heard the female beg him on with mewing growls.

His own mating seems but a paltry tryst
in the cold spring with his scruffy vixen
and again the duty of the hunt. Out here,
he must guard the whining hangers-on
of last year's brood and tolerate
the needle-teeth of this year's whining kits.

The fox trots by and notes the big male never shares
his cage with cubs. The lion, the fox knows,
as much as a fox can know such things, that
the lion lives without obligations.

The lion fixes his gaze on some lost
savanna where impala dance. The red fox
trots by, lean and mangy, his fox smile
not a leer, but sly, as humans say.
He is certain that he is beast enough,
quick and clever for at least this good day.

MARK DEFOE

CONTRIBUTORS

Megan Adams is a Ph.D. candidate in rhetoric and composition at Bowling Green State University. Her research interests include Appalachian studies, digital storytelling, and community activism. She hopes her scholarly and personal work can help to erase rural stereotypes and uplift Appalachian culture.

James Braziel is the author of two novels: *Birmingham, 35 Miles* and *Snakeskin Road*. His shorter work has appeared in the *New York Times, Southern Humanities Review*, and *Chattahoochee Review*, among other places. He lives in North Alabama with his wife, poet Tina Mozelle Braziel.

Samantha Lynn Cole is a native of Lee County, Kentucky, who graduated from Berea College. Berea is now her home. There, she writes, works, and bakes.

Mark DeFoe's poems have recently appeared in *ABZ, Cold Mountain Review, Notre Dame Review, Café Review, Saranac Review, South Carolina Review,* and other magazines. He teaches in West Virginia Wesleyan's MFA in Writing Program.

Grace Toney Edwards is professor emeritus of Appalachian Studies and English at Radford University. Dr. Edwards was the founder and director of the Appalachian Regional Studies Center at Radford, from which she retired after thirty years of teaching and administrative work. She is senior editor of *A Handbook to Appalachia: An Introduction to the Region* and co-editor of the literature section of *The Encyclopedia of Appalachia*.

Kari Gunter-Seymour is a graphic designer, photographer, poet and women's rights advocate. She has received various awards for her photography and has been published in *The Sun Magazine, Riverwind*, and *The Awakening*. She is the founder and curator of the Women of Appalachia Events, which celebrate Appalachian Ohio's visual, literary, and performing women artists.

Leah Hampton lives in Waynesville, North Carolina, and chairs the developmental studies program at A-B Tech College in Asheville. Her work has appeared in *North Carolina Literary Review, The Wallace Stevens Journal*, and elsewhere. Research for her short story "Queen" was supported in part by a Western North Carolina Regional Arts Project Grant from the Haywood County Arts Council.

Pauletta Hansel is a writer, teacher, and author of four poetry collections, most recently *The Lives We Live in Houses* and *What I Did There*; her fifth collection, *Tangle*, is forthcoming. She is co-editor of *Pine Mountain Sand & Gravel*, the literary publication of Southern Appalachian Writers Cooperative.

Jeanne Marie Hibberd serves as development and communications director for Hindman Settlement School, where she is actively involved in planning and coordinating the annual Appalachian Writers Workshop. An accomplished photographer, Hibberd has spent the last two decades working with communities, nonprofits, civic groups and businesses, primarily in Kentucky and Appalachia.

A native of upper East Tennessee, **Jane Hicks** is an award-winning poet and quilter. Her poetry has appeared in journals and numerous anthologies, and her first book, *Blood and Bone Remember*, was nominated for and won several awards. Her "literary quilts" illustrate the works of playwright Jo Carson and novelists Sharyn McCrumb and Silas House. The University Press of Kentucky will publish her latest poetry book, *Driving with the Dead*, in the fall of 2014.

Richard E. Joines was born in the Smokies, grew up in Nashville, and has worked and studied throughout the South. He now writes, teaches, and rides his bike in Denton, Texas. His poems and book reviews have appeared in *The Rumpus, Southern Humanities Review, American Literary Review, Quarterly West, Tusculum Review, Contemporary Poetry Review, Byrn Mawr Classical Review*, and in a chapbook, *Paradeisos*.

Sonja Livingston's latest book, *Queen of the Fall*, is forthcoming. Her first book, Ghostbread, won an AWP Prize for Creative Nonfiction. "Blue Kentucky Girl" is from a book-in-progress about little known historic women. Recent essays appear in *Arts & Letters, Bellingham*

Review, Brevity, The Seneca Review, and others. Livingston splits her time between New York and Memphis, where she teaches in the MFA Program at the University of Memphis.

Erica Abrams Locklear is an associate professor in the Literature and Language department at the University of North Carolina-Asheville who greatly appreciates the help John Inscoe and Wayne Caldwell offered her with this essay. She is the author of *Negotiating a Perilous Empowerment: Appalachian Women's Literacies* and has also published in *Appalachia in the Classroom, The Southern Literary Journal, North Carolina Literary Review,* and others.

George Ella Lyon's most recent books include *Many-Storied House: Poems*; *What Forest Knows* (a picture book); and *Voices from the March on Washington,* a collection of poetry for young adults co-written with J. Patrick Lewis. A native of Harlan County, Kentucky, Lyon is married to musician/writer Steve Lyon and has two grown sons. She makes her living as a freelance writer and teacher based in Lexington.

Linda Parsons Marion is an editor at the University of Tennessee and the author of three poetry collections, most recently, *Bound.* Her work has appeared in journals such as *The Georgia Review, Iowa Review, Southern Poetry Review,* and *Shenandoah*; Ted Kooser's syndicated column *American Life in Poetry;* and in numerous anthologies.

A.W. Marshall lives in Oklahoma but grew up on the beaches of Southern California. His work is published or forthcoming in *Red Wheelbarrow, TheNewerYork, Fiction Attic, Austin Review,* and *Vestal Review.* He received his MFA in Playwriting from University of Southern California and an MFA in Writing from Vermont College of Fine Arts. He is co-editor of *Piece Meal,* an online magazine that exclusively reviews poems and short stories from literary magazines.

Suzi Phillips is an amateur photographer living deep in a holler in Haywood County, North Carolina. "Gossip Girls" was also a finalist in the 2013 Appalachain Mountain Photography Competition. This is her first publication.

Charles A. Swanson is pastor of Melville Avenue Baptist Church and teaches dual enrollment college composition at the Academy for Engineering and Technology in Danville, Virginia. He is a graduate of Radford University with an M.A. in English, and has an MFA from Queens University-Charlotte. Swanson's collection *After the Garden: Selected Responses to the Psalms* and chapbook *Farm Life and Legend*, were both published in 2009.

Jessica D. Thompson's poems have appeared, or are forthcoming, in numerous journals across the country, among them *Atlanta Review, The Chaffin Journal, Tiferet Journal, The Sow's Ear,* and *The Midwest Quarterly*. She is the author of the chapbook *Bullets and Blank Bibles*, and was awarded the 2013 James Baker Hall Memorial Prize in Poetry by *New Southerner* and the 2014 *Kudzu* Poetry Prize.